Oxford
International
Resources

1

English
Student Book

Anna Yeomans
Liz Miles

OXFORD
UNIVERSITY PRESS

OXFORD
UNIVERSITY PRESS

Great Clarendon Street, Oxford, OX2 6DP, United Kingdom

Oxford University Press is a department of the University of Oxford. It furthers the University's objective of excellence in research, scholarship, and education by publishing worldwide. Oxford is a registered trade mark of Oxford University Press in the UK and in certain other countries.

British Library Cataloguing in Publication Data

Data available

ISBN 978-1-38-201979-8

10 9 8

Paper used in the production of this book is a natural, recyclable product made from wood grown in sustainable forests. The manufacturing process conforms to the environmental regulations of the country of origin.

Printed in India by Multivista Global Pvt. Ltd

Acknowledgements

The publisher and authors would like to thank the following for permission to use photographs and other copyright material:

Cover: Artwork by Dan Gartman. **Photos: p3(a):** Andrea Slatter/Shutterstock; **p3(b):** Krzysztof Odziomek/Shutterstock; **p20:** Liron Peer/Shutterstock; **p24(tl):** Ken Hurst/Shutterstock; **p24(tr):** imageBROKER/Alamy Stock Photo; **p24(b):** Peshkova/Shutterstock; **p25(t):** sarawut muensang/Shutterstock; **p25(tl):** Maksim Maksimovich/Shutterstock; **p25(tr):** asiandelight/Shutterstock; **p25(bl):** Oxford University Press; **p25(bcl):** Oxford University Press; **p25(bcr):** Oxford University Press; **p25(br):** Darkdiamond67/Shutterstock; **p28(tl):** Oxford University Press; **p28(bl):** Oxford University Press; **p29:** koblizeek/Shutterstock; **p30(tl):** pockygallery/Shutterstock; **p30(tr):** Tribalium/Shutterstock; **p30(bl):** NEGOVURA/Shutterstock; **p30(br):** Arcady/Shutterstock; **p31(tl):** Natalin*ka/Shutterstock; **p31(tr):** Anna Om/Shutterstock; **p31(c):** Rafal Olechowski/Shutterstock; **p31(bl):** Tim Graham/Hulton Archive/Getty Images; **p31(br):** Natee K Jindakum/Shutterstock; **p32:** kornnphoto/Shutterstock; **p34:** Rafal Olechowski/Shutterstock; **p37(l):** Natalin*ka/Shutterstock; **p37(m):** Rafal Olechowski/Shutterstock; **p37(r):** Natee K Jindakum/Shutterstock; **p37(bl):** Anna Om/Shutterstock; **p37(br):** Tim Graham/Hulton Archive/Getty Images; **p38:** Ian Andrews / Alamy Stock Photo; **p39(t):** PRASANNAPIX/Shutterstock; **p39(tm):** Pixel-Shot/Shutterstock; **p39(bm):** MaLija/Shutterstock; **p39(b):** Estudio Grafico Ve/Shutterstock; **p45:** Elvetica/Shutterstock; **p47(tl):** Foxys Forest Manufacture/Shutterstock; **p47(tr):** Nickola_Che/Shutterstock; **p47(bl):** images.etc/Shutterstock; **p47(br):** leonori/Shutterstock; **p53(t):** Milica011/Shutterstock; **p53(b):** Rich Carey/Shutterstock; **p54:** Larina Marina/Shutterstock; **p72(tl):** heliopix/Shutterstock; **p72(tml):** Liliya Butenko/Shutterstock; **p72(tmr):** Kitch Bain/Shutterstock; **p72(tr):** arka38/Shutterstock; **p73:** Willyam Bradberry/Shutterstock; **p74:** Shutterstock; **p75(t):** WaterFrame / Alamy Stock Photo; **p75(m):** Krzysztof Odziomek/Shutterstock; **p75(b):** Corbis/VCG/Getty Images; **p76:** Mark Conlin / VWPics / Alamy Stock Photo; **p77:** Shutterstock; **p78:** Krzysztof Odziomek/Shutterstock; **p80:** Willyam Bradberry/Shutterstock; **p81(m):** Oleksiy Maksymenko Photography/Alamy Stock Photo; **p81(b):** Arnold Media/Photodisc/Getty Images; **p82(t):** Terrance Klassen/Alamy Stock Photo; **p82(m):** OSTILL is Franck Camhi/Shutterstock; **p82(b):** Stéphane Bégoin; **p84:** Arnold Media/Photodisc/Getty Images; **p85:** jlbuyz/Shutterstock; **p94:** Wolfgang Kaehler/LightRocket/Getty Images; **p98:** lia.lait/Shuttertock; **p99(t):** Fulltimegipsy/Shutterstock;

p99(b): Em7/Shutterstock; **p113(l):** Paul Orr/Shutterstock; **p113(m):** Anna Om/Shutterstock; **p113(r):** Brian A Jackson/Shutterstock; **p114(tl):** Iakov Kalinin/Shutterstock; **p114(tr):** daniilphotos/Shutterstock; **p114(bl):** Lifestyle Travel Photo/Shutterstock.

Artwork by Dan Gartman, Joe Todd *Stanton*, Ilias Arahovits, Marine & Annalisa Durante, Elina Ellis, François Ruyer, Micha Archer, Victoria Assanelli, Alex Brychta, Alexandra Colombo, Hannah Cummings, Jacqui Davis, Nina De Polonia-Nil, David Dean, Jaqueline East, Daniela Geremia, D'Arcy Hipgrave, Tamara Joubert, Zack Mcloughlin, Patricia Moffat, Marcin Piewowarski, Andrew Painter, Caroline Romanet, Jane Smith, Meilo So, Alex Steele-Morgan, Nick Ward, Laura Watson, and Q2A Media Services Pvt. Ltd.

Hannah Cumming: *The Lost Stars* (Child's Play, 2011), copyright © Hannah Cumming 2011, reprinted by permission of Child's Play (International) Ltd.

John Foster: 'Poppadoms', first published in *Oxford Reading Tree: Food Poems* compiled by John Foster (OUP, 1993), copyright © John Foster 1993, reprinted by permission of the author.

Becca Heddle illustrated by Joe Todd-Stanton: *Glimmer* (Oxford Reading Buddy, OUP, 2019), reprinted by permission of Oxford University Press.

D'Arcy Hipgrave: 'My First Year in Vietnam' from *Slurping Soup and other confusions: true stories and activities to help third culture kids during transition* by Maryan Afnan Ahmad, Cherie Emigh, Ulrike Gemmer, Barbara Menezes, Kathryn Tonges and Lucinda Willshire, (2e, Summertime Publishing, 2013), www.slurpingsoup.com 2010, copyright © 2010 Slurping Soup and Other Confusions, reprinted by permission of the co-authors.

Richard James: 'Today I'm a Drummer' first published in *Oxford Reading Tree, Music Poems* compiled by John Foster (OUP, 1996), reprinted by permission of the author, Richard Edwards.

Laurie Krebs: *Off We Go To Mexico! An Adventure in the Sun* (Barefoot Books Ltd, 2006), text copyright © Laurie Krebs 2006, reprinted by permission of Barefoot Books, Inc.

Liz Miles: 'Puff' from *One, Two, Buckle My Shoe: Magical number Rhymes, old and new* (Award Publications, 2006), copyright © Liz Miles 2006, reprinted by permission of the author; Liz Miles illustrated by Meilo So: *The Magic Paintbrush: A Tale from China*, ORT Traditional Tales (OUP, 2011), text copyright © Liz Miles 2011, this adapted version copyright © Liz Miles 2015, illustrations copyright © Oxford University Press 2011, reprinted by permission of the author and Oxford University Press.

Tony Mitton: 'Tiny Diny', copyright © Tony Mitton 2001, from *Pip* (Scholastic, 2002), reprinted by permission of David Higham Associates Ltd for the author.

Nicola Moon: *Grandma's Glasses,* ORT Level 3 Snapdragons (OUP, 2004), copyright © Nicola Moon 2004, reprinted by permission of David Higham Associates Ltd for the author.

Jack Prelutsky: 'Late One Night in Kalamazoo' from *Ride a Purple Pelican* (Green Willow Books, 1986), copyright © Jack Prelutsky 1986, reprinted by permission of the publishers, HarperCollins Publishers, USA.

Michael Rosen: 'Diggedy-Do' from *Michael Rosen's Book of Nonsense* (Hodder Children's Books, 2008), copyright © Michael Rosen 1997, reprinted by permission of Peters Fraser & Dunlop Ltd (www.petersfraserdunlop.com) on behalf of the author.

Judy Sierra: 'A Hatchling's Song' from *Antarctic Antics: A Book of Penguin Poems* (Voyager Paperbacks, 2003), text copyright © Judy Sierra 1998, reprinted by permission of Houghton Mifflin Harcourt Publishing Company. All rights reserved.

Any third-party use of this material, outside of this publication, is prohibited. Interested parties should apply to the copyright holders indicated in each case.

Every effort has been made to contact copyright holders of material reproduced in this book. Any omissions will be rectified in subsequent printings if notice is given to the publisher.

The manufacturer's authorised representative in the EU for product safety is Oxford University Press España S.A. of el Parque Empresarial San Fernando de Henares, Avenida de Castilla, 2–28830 Madrid (www.oup.es/en).

Contents

Arctic Ocean

United Kingdom

North America

Atlantic Ocean

USA

Mexico

Pacific Ocean

In this book you'll find stories, poems and facts from these places. Have a look!

South America

4

Czech Republic

Europe

China

Asia

frica

Vietnam

Indian Ocean

Australia

Oceania

Southern Ocean

Antarctica

Unit contents

Unit	Theme	Reading and comprehension	Writing
1	**At home**	**Fiction** Narrative with a familiar setting *Grandma's Glasses*	• Fiction • Writing about a familiar experience • Describing a person or animal
2	**Show me, tell me**	**Non-fiction** Signs, labels and instructions, *Our senses, The human body*	• Non-fiction • Writing signs • Drawing and labelling items
3	**Everyday poems**	**Poems** 'Diggedy-Do', 'Today I'm a Drummer', 'Poppadoms'	• Poetry • Writing rhyming words
4	**Make the world a better place**	**Fiction** *The Magic Paintbrush*	• Fiction • Writing sentences about a story • Writing a story blurb
5	**Water world**	**Non-fiction** Reports and dictionaries *A–Z of the Sea, Ocean Sharks, Sea Transport*	• Non-fiction • Writing labels • Writing sentences
6	**Creatures big and small**	**Poems** Simple rhymes and poems 'Puff!', 'Late One Night in Kalamazoo', 'A Hatchling's Song', 'Tiny Diny'	• Poetry • Writing rhyming words
7	**Stories about our world**	**Fiction** narrative *The Lost Stars*	• Fiction • Writing sentences
8	**About my life**	**Non-fiction** Recounts *My First Year in Vietnam was Weird, Alex Brychta – a Biography*	• Non-fiction • Writing a recount
9	**Poems that tell a story**	**Poem** Narrative poem 'Off We Go To Mexico!'	• Poetry • Writing a narrative poem

Unit	Language, grammar, spelling, vocabulary, punctuation	Phonics	Speaking and listening
1	• Adjectives • Sentence punctuation: capital letters and full stops	• Initial letter sounds • Blend sounds	• Listening and confident talking in turns • Questions – developing ideas and extending understanding • Reciting the alphabet
2	• New words in context • Rhyming words • Verbs • Sentence punctuation: capital letters and full stops	• Initial letter sounds • Blend sounds • Digraph, **ch**	• Listening and confident talking in turns • Questions – developing ideas and extending understanding
3	• Rhyming words • New words in context • Features of poetry genre • Capital letter for **I**	• Blend sounds • Digraphs, **sh**, **ch** • Initial letter sounds	• Listening and confident talking in turns • Reciting poems • Expressing opinions • Questions – developing ideas and extending understanding
4	• New words in context • Adjectives • Sentence punctuation: capital letters and full stops	• Blend sounds • Digraphs, **ch**, **sh**, **th** • Long vowel phonemes, **/ee/ /oo/ /ai/**	• Listening and confident talking in turns • Questions – developing ideas and extending understanding • Retelling stories • Confident talking in discussion
5	• Link words to meaning • Common word endings, **-ing**, **-s** • New words in context • Verbs	• Blend sounds • Digraph, **sh**	• Confident talking in discussion • Questions – developing ideas and extending understanding • Listening and confident talking in turns
6	• Rhyming words • Common word endings, **-ed**, **-ing** • New words in context • Describing words (adjectives) • Verbs	• Blend sounds • Long vowel phoneme **/oo/** • Digraph, **sh**	• Expressing opinions • Listening and confident talking in turns • Reciting poems • Questions – developing ideas and extending understanding
7	• New words in context • Descriptions • Sentence punctuation: capital letters and full stops • Compound words	• Blend sounds • Long vowel phonemes, **/ea/ /ee/ /y/ /igh/ /oo/**	• Questions – developing ideas and extending understanding • Organisation of ideas • Listening and confident talking in turns • Confident talking in discussion • Retelling stories
8	• New words in context • Sentence punctuation: capital letters and full stops • Joining sentences with **and** • Compound words • Common word endings, **-s**, **-ing**, **-ed** • Language and features of recounts • Opposites with **un-**	• Blend sounds	• Questions – developing ideas and extending understanding • Organization of ideas • Questions – developing ideas and extending understanding
9	• New words in context • Adjectives • Ordering sentences • Rhyming words • Verbs	• Long vowel phoneme, **/ee/** • Blend sounds	• Listening and confident talking in turns • Confident talking in discussion • Questions – developing ideas and extending understanding

1 At home

Grandpa

Mum

Lin

Dad

Talk time

1 Look at the pictures. What can you see?

2 Who lives in your home?

3 Ask a partner about the people in their family. Answer questions about the people in your family.

- Talk about your family
- Listen to others

A Who is in your family? Draw a picture of them and write their names.

B Think of one word to describe each member of your family. Use the words in the box below to help you.

> kind   helpful   happy   funny
> busy   loving   old   young

Glossary

kind friendly and ready to help other people
helpful offering help to others
happy feeling pleased about something
funny something that makes you laugh

C

1 What does each person in your family like doing? Tell a partner.

2 Write a sentence about what each person likes doing.

My mum likes … .

My dad likes … .

My brother likes … .

My sister likes … .

painting   cooking

reading   gardening

running   eating

Grandma's Glasses

Nicola Moon

Grandma lost her **glasses**.

Glossary

glasses a frame with pieces of glass, worn over the eyes to help people see

She looked under the table and she saw her pen.

That's my pen!

Grandpa came to help.

He looked in the **drawer** and he found his book.

That's my book!

Glossary

drawer a piece of furniture that pulls out where you can keep things

Harry looked too. He saw his **comic** on the table.

Glossary

comic a story told with pictures

Mina looked under the **cushion**. She saw her teddy.

Hello teddy!

Glossary

cushion a soft pillow for chairs and sofas

Then Mum came to help.

She looked behind the **curtains**. She found Mina's lost **shoe**.

It's your lost shoe!

Glossary

curtains two cloths which can be pulled over a window

shoe a covering for the foot

Everyone looked and looked. They saw lots of things, but … no glasses.

Then Harry said, "I can see Grandma's glasses. They are on her head!"

● Find information in a story

A Read and respond

1 What did Grandma lose? Point to the picture and say the word.

| shoe | glasses | pen |

2 Where did Grandpa find his book?
Point to the picture and say the phrase.

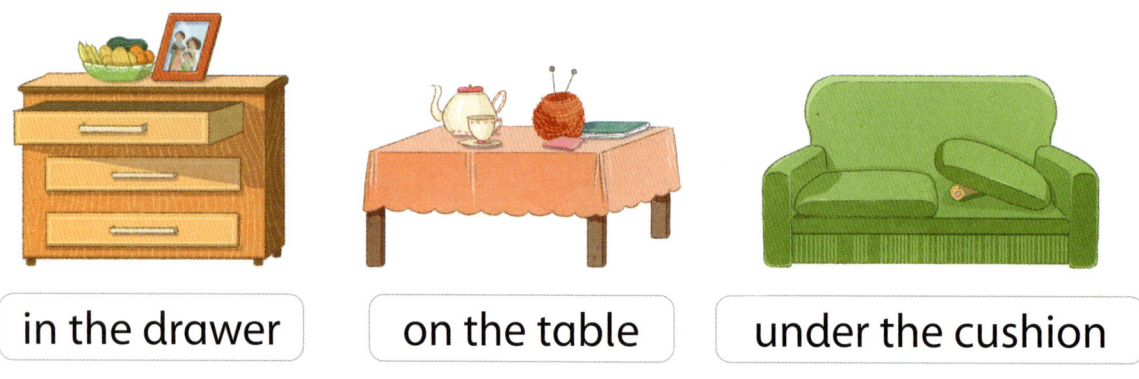

| in the drawer | on the table | under the cushion |

3 What had Mina lost? Point to the picture and say the word.

| shoe | cup | pen |

• Talk about characters

B

1 Who found Mina's shoe? Say the name, then write it.

2 Who found a book? Say the name, then write it.

3 How did Grandma feel when she found her glasses on her head? Tell a partner.

4 How did Mina feel when she found her teddy? Tell a partner.

Learning tip
You can copy the name from the story.

5 In pairs, take it in turns to be Mina. Pretend you have found your teddy. What do you say and do?

- Spell words from the story
- Use capital letters

A

1 Write the names of three people from the story. Start each name with a capital letter.

Language tip
Names always start with a **capital letter**.

2 Work with a partner. Unjumble the words from the story and write them.

tedyd

galsess

eosh

koob

Read your answers aloud to check your spelling.

● Look at the sounds that words begin with

1 Work with a partner. Find words in the story that begin with these letters: **p g c t s h**. Write them down.

2 Write another word that begins with each of these letters: **p g c t s h**.

3 Look at the pictures below and say the word aloud. Tell a partner what sound each word begins with.

4 Work with a partner. Take turns to choose a letter and say its letter name aloud. Ask a partner to point to it.

a b c d e f g
h i j k l m n
o p q r s t u
v w x y z

5 Take turns to say a word. Ask a partner to point to the letter it begins with.

6 Say or sing the alphabet together. Clap your hands as you say each letter.

• Use capital letters and full stops

1 Write the sentence below. Add two capital letters and one full stop.

mum found mina's shoe behind the curtain

2 Write a sentence about where Harry found Grandma's glasses. Remember to add the full stop and capital letters.

3 Have you ever lost anything? Tell a partner about it.

4 Write a sentence about what you lost and where you found it.

I lost my … .

I found it … .

Language tip
Sentences start with a capital letter and end with a **full stop**.

5 Swap sentences with a partner. Check your partner's writing. Have they used a capital letter and a full stop?

- Describe people
- Write about being helpful
- Talk about a question

Part 1

1 We looked at words to describe people: *kind, helpful, happy, funny*. Tell a partner some other words to describe people.

2 Grandma's family were helpful. Tell a partner about a time when you were helpful.

3 Write a sentence about a time when you were helpful.

I was helpful when I … .

Examples:

I was helpful when I set the table.

I was helpful when I went to the shop.

4 Read your partner's sentence. Have they remembered a capital letter and a full stop?

?

Why is it important to be kind and helpful? Talk about a time when someone was kind or helpful to you. How did it make you feel?

- Write about a person or an animal
- Tell a story

Part 2

1 Draw a picture of a person or an animal who is kind, helpful, happy or funny.

kind

helpful

happy

funny

2 Tell a partner about that person or animal.
- What is their name?
- What do they do?

3 Write a sentence about them.

4 Check your sentence for spelling, capital letters and full stops.

5 Tell a partner a story about the person or animal.

Stretch zone

Write two sentences from your story about a person or an animal who is kind, helpful, happy or funny.

Language tip
Adjectives help you to describe people and things. For example: The teacher is **kind**. She is a **kind** teacher. Amina is **funny**. She makes me laugh.

2 Show me, tell me

A

B

Talk time

1 Where would you see signs like the ones in **A**? What is each sign saying?

2 Is the book in **B** a storybook or a book that shows you how to do something?

3 Tell a partner about a book you have read that tells you how to do something.

- Talk about signs and labels
- Listen to others

A Signs are in lots of different places. Draw a picture of a sign you have seen before. Tell a partner what it shows you.

B Look at the three signs below. Tell a partner who needs each sign and why they need it.

C

1 Look at the book covers with a partner. Which books are stories?

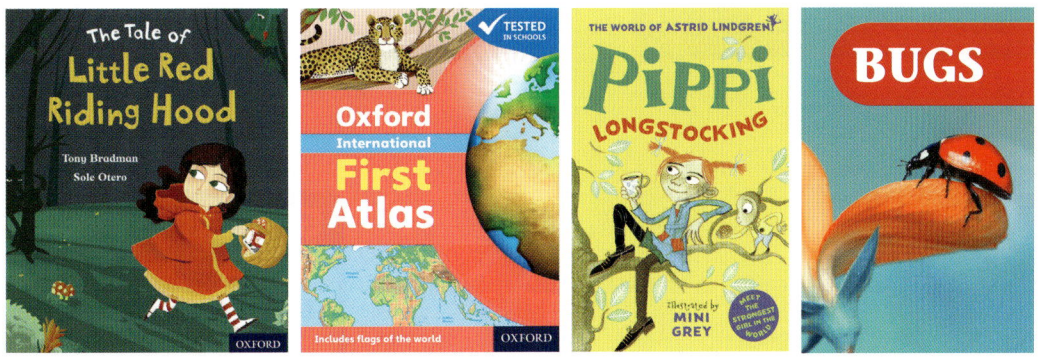

2 Tell a partner which books are about real life. How do you know?

Signs show us where to go in.

Signs tell us what to do.

In the classroom, signs help us to find things.

Signs tell us where we must **not** go.

Glossary

signs writing or pictures that tell or show people something

● Talk about signs

A Read and respond

Talk to a partner about these signs.

1 Which sign tells you to do something?

2 Which sign shows you where to go?

B Which sign tells you where you can read a book? Point to it and read it aloud.

C **What do you think?**

1 Book covers help us to know what the book is about. Which of these books would you like to read? Tell a partner why.

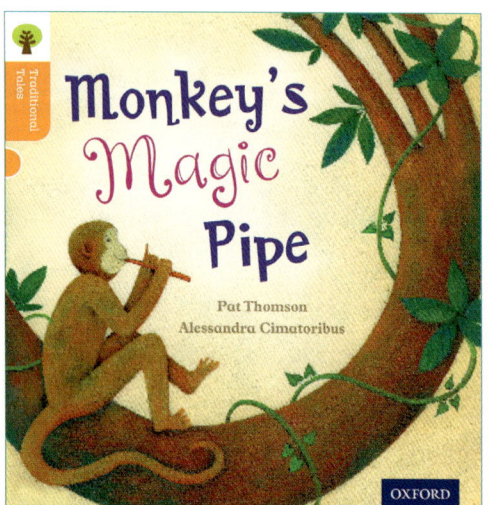

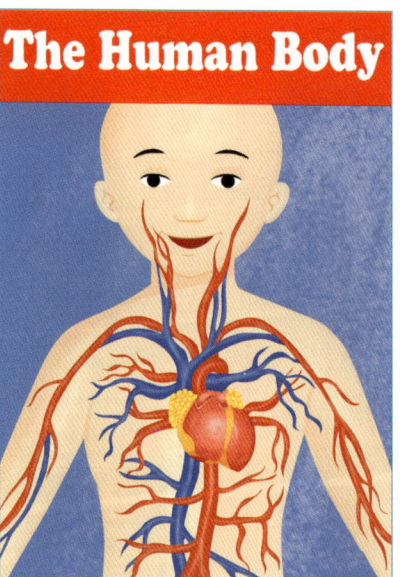

2 Tell a partner whether you prefer storybooks or books about real life. Why?

- Find sounds at the start of words
- Use capital letters

A Read the words below. Find three words that start with the same sound. Write them down.

> book   stop   exit   staff
> hand   sign

B Copy the signs. Add in the missing letters to complete the words.

> e   h   o

Language tip
Signs don't have a **full stop** at the end.

Wash your __ands

No __ntry

Staff __nly

BOOKS

Danger
Deep Water

C Signs start with capital letters. Copy the words and add capital letters.

___ ook corner

___ anger

___ top

STOP

- Talk about signs
- Write a sign

Part 1

Tell a partner what each sign is telling you to do, or not to do.

Language tip
Remember to start each sentence with a **capital letter** and add a **full stop** at the end.

Part 2

With a partner, write your own sign to put on a door in your school.

● Read about the senses

Our senses

see

1

2

hear

3

smell

4

touch

taste

5

We have five senses.

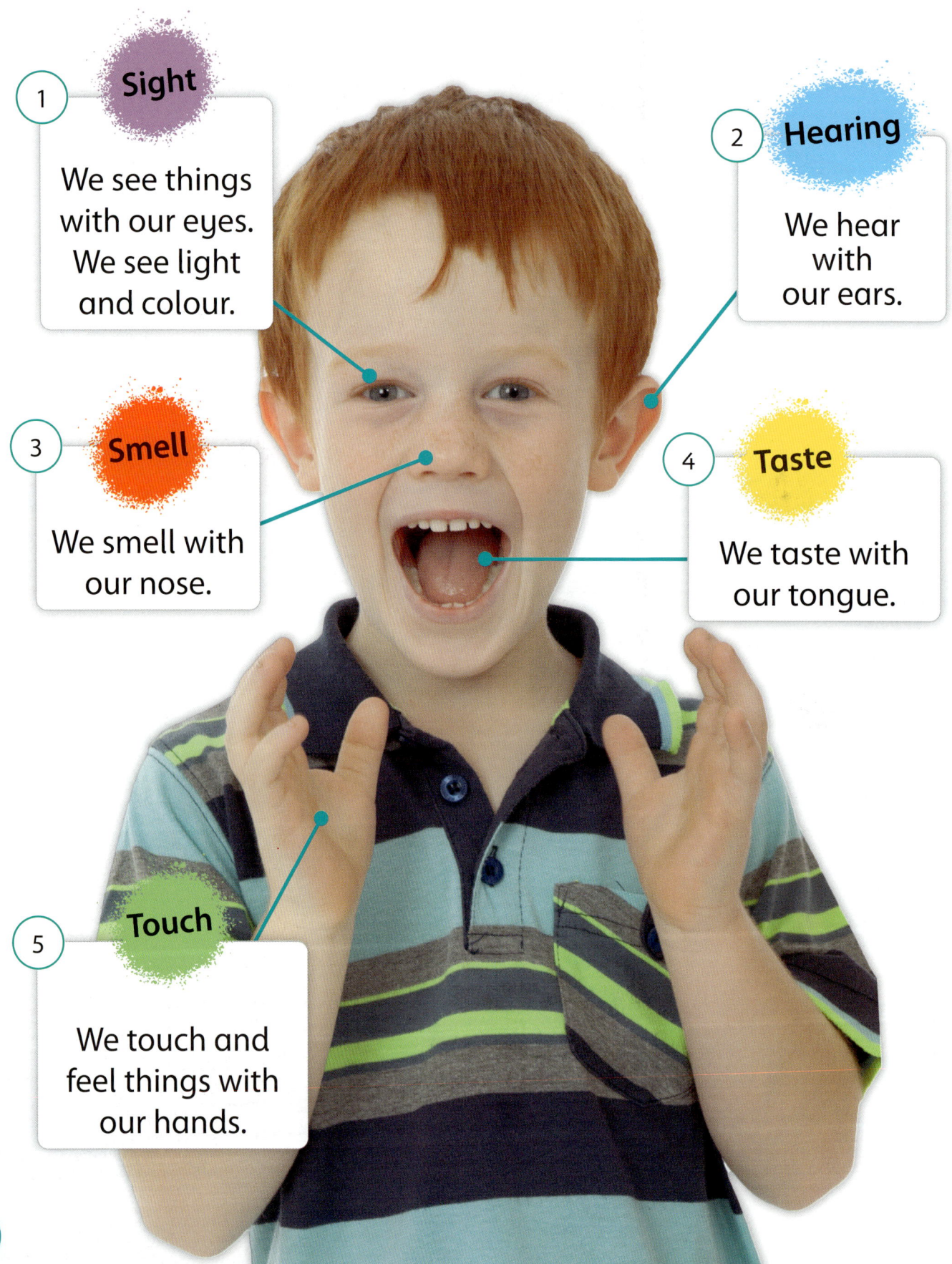

1 **Sight**

We see things with our eyes. We see light and colour.

2 **Hearing**

We hear with our ears.

3 **Smell**

We smell with our nose.

4 **Taste**

We taste with our tongue.

5 **Touch**

We touch and feel things with our hands.

- Find information in a text
- Find information in labels

A Read and respond

1 How many senses are there?

2 What can you do with your hands?
Point to the word and say it.

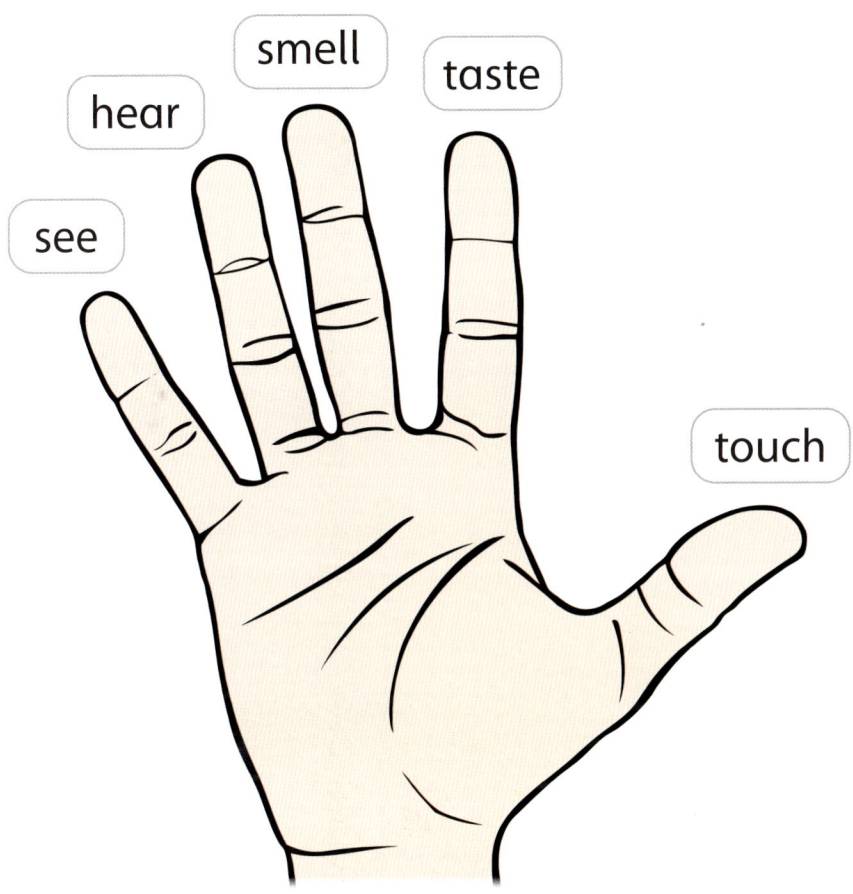

smell

taste

hear

see

touch

B Point to your nose. Tell a partner what you can do with your nose.

C Which sense is most important to you? Tell a partner why.

sight   hearing   smell   taste   touch

- Look at the sound /**ch**/
- Find rhyming words

A

1   On page 31, find a word that has the same end spelling as **lun<u>ch</u>**.

2   Point to it and say it. Write it down.

B   These letters are mixed up. Which sense do they spell? Write the word.

l   m   e   s   l

C   Read the sentence below. Point to the words that rhyme in each sentence.

I **<u>hear</u>** with my **e<u>ar</u>**.

I can see a tree.

I spot a bright light.

Honey is a treat; it tastes sweet.

Language tip
Words that **rhyme** sound the same, like **fun** and **run**.

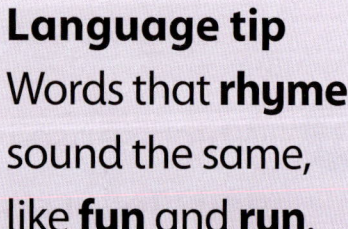

● Label the human body

The human body

1 Draw a picture of the human body.

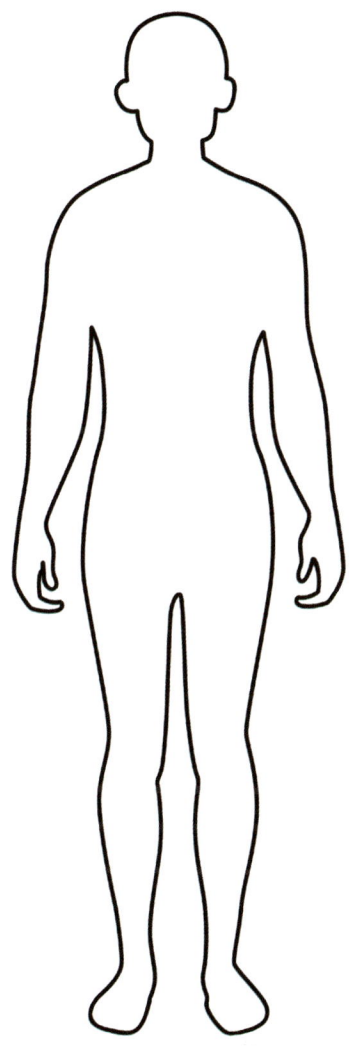

Language tip
Words that name things are called **nouns**.

2 Take turns to point to a body part and ask a partner to name it.

3 Read these words and point to them on your picture.

> **head**   **arm**   **leg**   **eyes**   **nose**
> **mouth**   **face**   **chest**   **foot**   **hand**

B

1 Work with a partner. Write the words from the box below on your picture. Add the words next to the correct body part.

head	**arm**	**leg**	**eyes**	**nose**
mouth	**face**	**chest**	**foot**	**hand**

2 Copy the words below in your notebook. Add the missing letters to complete the body parts.

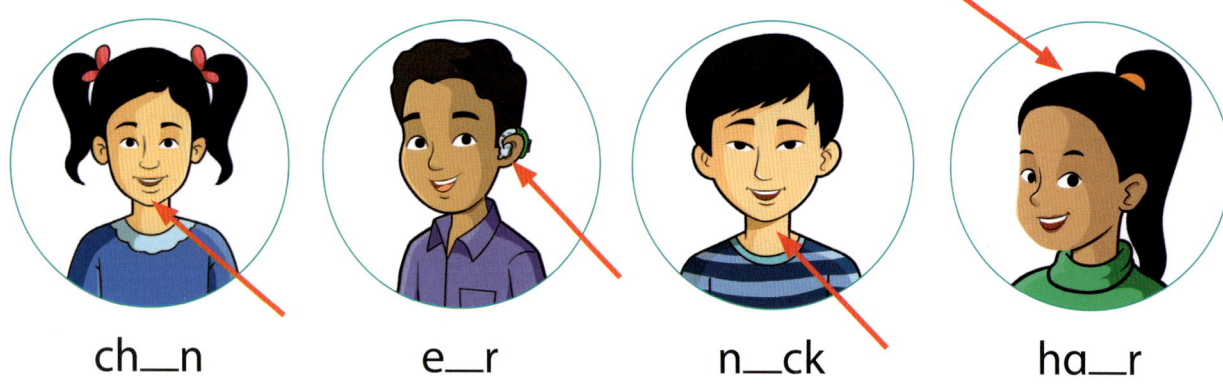

ch__n   e__r   n__ck   ha__r

3 Add the words as labels to your picture.

4 Look at the activities in the box. Which sense does each one use? Tell a partner.

stroke a pet   sniff a flower

eat an ice cream

play in the playground

● Use capital letters and full stops

1 Label three more body parts on your picture.

2 Copy these sentences. Add two full stops and two capital letters.

we see things with our eyes we see light and colour

3 Add labels to your picture to show which body parts we use to: see, hear, smell, taste and touch.

- Talk about actions
- Use doing words

 A

1 Which of these activities do you like to do?

> **run jump sing dance skip play football**

2 Tell a partner why you like these activities.

 B

1 One person says a verb.

2 The rest of the group do the action.

3 The speaker chooses the next person to say a verb.

4 Tell a partner which part of your body you used to do each action.

Language tip
Doing words are called **verbs**.

- Talk about staying healthy
- Talk about a question

C   What do you think?

1   Tell a partner what things a person can do to keep healthy.

2   What things do you do to keep your body healthy?

?

Why is it important to be fit and healthy? Talk about whose job it is to make sure you stay healthy.

Stretch zone

Make a poster for your class showing ways we can stay healthy.
Think about:
- what to eat
- fun activities to keep you healthy
- other ways we can stay healthy.

Diggedy-Do

Diggedy-do

Diggedy-do

The train is late

what shall we do?

Diggedy-do

Diggedy-do

The train is late

what a **to-do**.

Grandpa coughed

and the wheels fell off.

Diggedy-do

Diggedy-do.

What's the opposite of Diggedy-do?

Diggedy-don't!

Michael Rosen

Glossary

to-do a commotion or fuss

Talk time

1 Do you have a hobby, like model trains?

2 Why do you enjoy this hobby?

3 Read the poem aloud together.

4 What does it sound like?

- Talk about hobbies
- Listen to others
- Read a poem

Language tip
Diggedy-do is a word that copies a sound. Other words that copy sounds are **quack**, **splash**, **squeak**.

41

A Read and respond

1 What did Grandpa do? Tell a partner.

> **He sneezed.**   **He coughed.**
> **He went to bed.**

B

1 What made the wheels fall off? Tell a partner.

> **the speed of the train**
> **the wobbly track**   **Grandpa's cough**

2 Which word has the same sound as **off**? Point to the word and say it with a partner.

C What do you think?

1 Read the poem aloud again with a partner.

2 Why do you think the poet repeats the words **diggedy-do**? What sound in the poem is it copying?

> **the train rushing along**
> **a clock ticking**   **Grandpa coughing**

- Look at the letters **sh**
- Find rhyming words

A In the poem, find a word that has the same beginning spelling as **sh**op. Say it with a partner and write it down.

Language tip
Words that **rhyme** sound the same, like **fun** and **run**.

B Find words in the poem that rhyme with these.

| brain | date | feels |

C Find these words from the poem in the word search.

| fell | off | and | the | we |

a	n	d	o	s
w	e	g	a	j
o	o	f	f	h
b	f	e	l	l
t	h	e	z	n

- Read a poem
- Talk about sounds
- Listen to others

Today I'm a Drummer

Today I'm a drummer,
I'm drumming everywhere,
I'm drumming on the table-top,
I'm drumming on the chair,
I'm drumming on the biscuit tin,
I'm drumming on the bread,
I'll drum my drums till evening comes,
And then I'll drum in bed.

Richard James

Talk time

1 What sound does a drum make?
2 Join in with the poem and use your hands to make a drumming sound in time with the poem.

44

A Read and respond

What sort of tin does the drummer drum on? Tell a partner.

> **a biscuit tin**   **a bread tin**
> **a table-top tin**

B

Where will the drummer drum at the end of the day? Tell a partner.

> **on the table**   **on the biscuit tin**
> **in bed**

C What do you think?

With a partner write a list of where else in this house you could drum.

- Look at the sound **/ch/**
- Find words that rhyme

 A Work with a partner. In the poem, find a word that has the same beginning sound as **ch**eese. Write it down.

 B

1 Find words in the poem that rhyme with these words. Write them down.

> **everywhere   bread**

2 Underline the sounds that sound the same.

Language tip
The **rhyming words** are always at the end of a line.

C

1 Find the different words in the poem that start with **drum**.

2 Write the words and underline **drum** in each word.

●Talk about food

Talk time

1 What foods do you like to eat?

2 What is your favourite food?

3 Why do you like it?

- Read a poem
- Learn new words
- Use a glossary

Poppadoms

Poppadoms, poppadoms,
plain or full of spice.

Poppadoms, poppadoms,
with chicken and rice.

Crispy hot poppadoms
to crunch and chew.

A plateful of poppadoms
just for me and you.

John Foster

Glossary

poppadoms large circular pieces of thin, fried, crispy bread

48

A Read and respond

Write two words from the poem that rhyme.

B Read and respond

Which set of words is about eating a poppadom? Tell a partner.

> **chicken and rice**   **me and you**
>
> **crunch and chew**

C What do you think?

1 With a partner, clap the beat of the poem as you read it aloud.

2 Talk about what makes it a good poem. Tell your partner what you like about it.

Language tip
The beat of a poem is called the **rhythm**.

- Find words with the sound **/ch/**
- Find adjectives
- Find sounds at the start of words

 A

1 Which three words have the **/ch/** sound sound in them? Point to them and say them with a partner.

> **chew   poppadom   chicken   crunch   rice**

 B

1 Find two words in the poem that are used to describe the poppadoms. Write them down.

2 Tell a partner what the first sound is in each of the words you have written down.

C

1 Think of two words to describe your favourite food.

2 Say them aloud. What sound does each of them start with?

Language tip
A word that describes something is called an **adjective**.

 50

Part 1

1 Copy the sentences. Finish each line with a word that makes a rhyme. Choose from the words in the box.

> **you   fish   hot   toast   nice**

What's in the pot?
It's for dinner and it's … .

Is it steamy white rice?
It's something very … .

Is it chilli or stew?
It's something just for … .

Is it chicken roast?
No, and it's not butter on … .

Is it my favourite dish?
Yes, it's curry with … .

2 Tell a partner about your favourite dish.

Part 2

1 Talk with a partner about foods you like to eat.

2 Write some sentences about foods you like to eat.

I like to eat _____ **for breakfast.**

I like to eat _____ **for lunch.**

I like to eat _____ **for dinner.**

- Write sentences
- Use a capital letter for **I**
- Talk about a question

Language tip
We always use a **capital letter** for **I** when we mean ourselves.

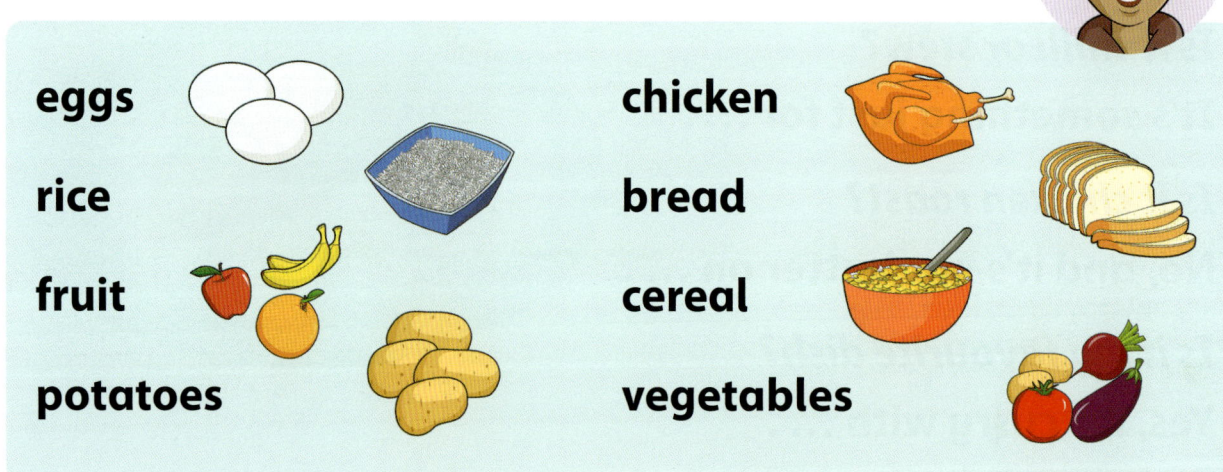

eggs

rice

fruit

potatoes

chicken

bread

cereal

vegetables

Stretch zone

Find a poem you like in one of your class books. Find someone to read it with you. Talk about the poem together.

?

Why should we try new food? Talk about a time you tried a new food. Did you like it? Why? Why not?

4 Make the world a better place

Talk time

1 Look at the pictures. What can you see?

2 What do you think life is like for the people and animals that live here?

- Talk about the world
- Say what might happen next

A Read the sentences below. Talk to a partner to decide whether they are true or false.

Everyone in the world has enough food to eat.

Plastic is polluting the oceans.

Trees are important for the air around us.

All people in the world have the same amount of money.

B Look at the pictures in the story on the next page.

What do you think the story will be about? How do you know?

- Read a story
- Learn new words
- Use a glossary

The Magic Paintbrush

A tale from China

Retold by Liz Miles

Long ago in a tiny village in China lived a young man called Ho. Every day, Ho worked for a rich farmer.

The farmer did not pay him much. Ho had only dry bread to eat.

One day a very thin, old man came up the lane. He looked hungry. Ho gave his bread to the man.

Take this.

"Thank you," said the man. He gave Ho a gift. It was a golden paintbrush.

Ho made paints from plants, berries and mud.

This is a magic paintbrush!

"What shall I paint?" thought Ho. He began to paint some hay. The hay became **real**!

Glossary

real something you can touch or see and is not made up or imaginary

56

- Find information in a story
- Talk about characters
- Make a prediction

A Read and respond

1 What did Ho give to the old man?

> **gold   a paintbrush   bread**

2 Tell a partner why you think he did this.

Take this.

B Read and respond

1 What did the old man give to Ho?

> **gold   a paintbrush   bread**

2 Tell a partner why you think he did this.

C What do you think?

Tell a partner what you think might happen next.

The sun was hot. The stream was dry. So Ho painted a blue stream.

The stream became real! Now the people and the animals had water to drink.

The rich farmer had lots of food to eat. But the children and **workers** were hungry.

Glossary

workers people who do jobs

Ho painted lots of food.
It became real!

He painted...

a wheel...

a bucket...

and some clothes.

- Find information in a story
- Talk about feelings

A Read and respond

How did Ho know the paintbrush was magic? Tell a partner.

B How did Ho help the people? Tell a partner.

C What do you think?

How do you think the people felt? Tell a partner.

happy   excited   sad   worried

- Read a story
- Learn new words
- Use a glossary

The farmer was **greedy**.

Glossary

greedy someone who wants more money or food than they need

"Paint me a mountain of gold!" ordered the farmer.

Ho painted the mountain of gold. He painted a blue sea all around it. The gold and the sea became real.

The farmer was angry.

"I cannot swim! Why did you paint the sea!" he shouted.

"I will paint a ship for you," said Ho. The ship became real.

The farmer set off in the ship.

"When I get back, you will paint everything I want. The world will be mine!" he laughed.

But Ho painted a **gale**. The gale became real. It took the farmer far, far away.

Glossary

gale a very strong wind

Ho returned to the farm. He painted things for those who were kind and good to others.

The rich farmer was never seen again.

63

- Look at the parts of a story
- Talk about feelings

A Read and respond

1 Stories often have a good character and a bad character. Who is the good character in this story? Who is the bad character? Tell a partner.

2 Tell a partner what happens at the beginning, middle and end of this story. Use the pictures to help you.

Language tip
Good characters in stories are called **heroes** or **heroines**.
Bad characters are called **villains**.

3 Talk to a partner about how you feel at the end of the story. Why?

• Find information in a story

1 What country is the story set in? Tell a partner.

Japan   China   Australia

2 Write three things that Ho painted.

3 Why did Ho paint a gale? Tell a partner.

- Talk about a character
- Talk about ideas

C What do you think?

1 How did Ho make the world a better place? Tell a partner.

2 What sort of boy do you think Ho is?

> **unkind   helpful   selfish   kind**

3 If you had a magic paintbrush, what would you paint? Why? Tell a partner, then write a sentence.

I would paint a … .

4 If you could make the world a better place, what would you do? Tell a partner and then write a sentence.

To make the world a better place I would … .

- Find words with the sounds **ch**, **sh** and **th**
- Find words with the sounds **/ee/**, **/oo/** and **/ai/**

A

1   Practise saying these sounds:
/ch/ /sh/ /th/

2   Find **ch** or **sh** or **th** in these words. Point to them and say the words with a partner.

> brush   China   much   shall
> children   shouted   thin   ship

B

1   Practise saying these sounds:
/ee/ /oo/ /ai/

2   Write the words with **ee**, **oo** and **ai** from the box below. Write in a chart like the one on page 68.

> greedy   paint   seen   wheel
> again   food   paintbrush

Language tip
Two letters together can make one sound, such as **ch** in ri**ch**, **th** in **th**in and **sh** in paintbru**sh**.

ee words	oo words	ai words
greedy		

Learning tip
You can copy this chart to help you.

C

1 Find three words with the **/ai/** sound, as in **tail**, from the story and write them down.

2 Now add two **ai** words of your own.

- Write sentences
- Retell a story
- Talk about a question

Part 1

1 Write a sentence for each picture about Ho. Remember to use capital letters and full stops.

2 Use the sentences to retell the story to a partner.

Ho worked ...

The old man ...

Language tip
Remember to use a **capital letter** at the beginning of a sentence and a **full stop** at the end. Capital letters should also be used for people's names.

Ho made paints with ...

Ho painted ...

?

Ho used his magic paintbrush to make the world a better place.
Can one person help to make the world a better place?

● Write a story blurb

Part 2

The writing below is a blurb. Copy the blurb and fill in the missing words with words from the box.

| paints | Ho | China | story |

Learning tip
A **blurb** is on the back of a book. It tells the reader what the book is about.

The Magic Paintbrush

The Magic Paintbrush is a traditional

_____ **set in** _____ .

An old man gives _____ **a gift.**

It is a magic paintbrush! Ho _____

lots of things and they become real!

Stretch zone

1. Ho is good at painting. What are you good at? Tell a partner.
2. Draw a picture and write two sentences about something you are good at.

5 Water world

A

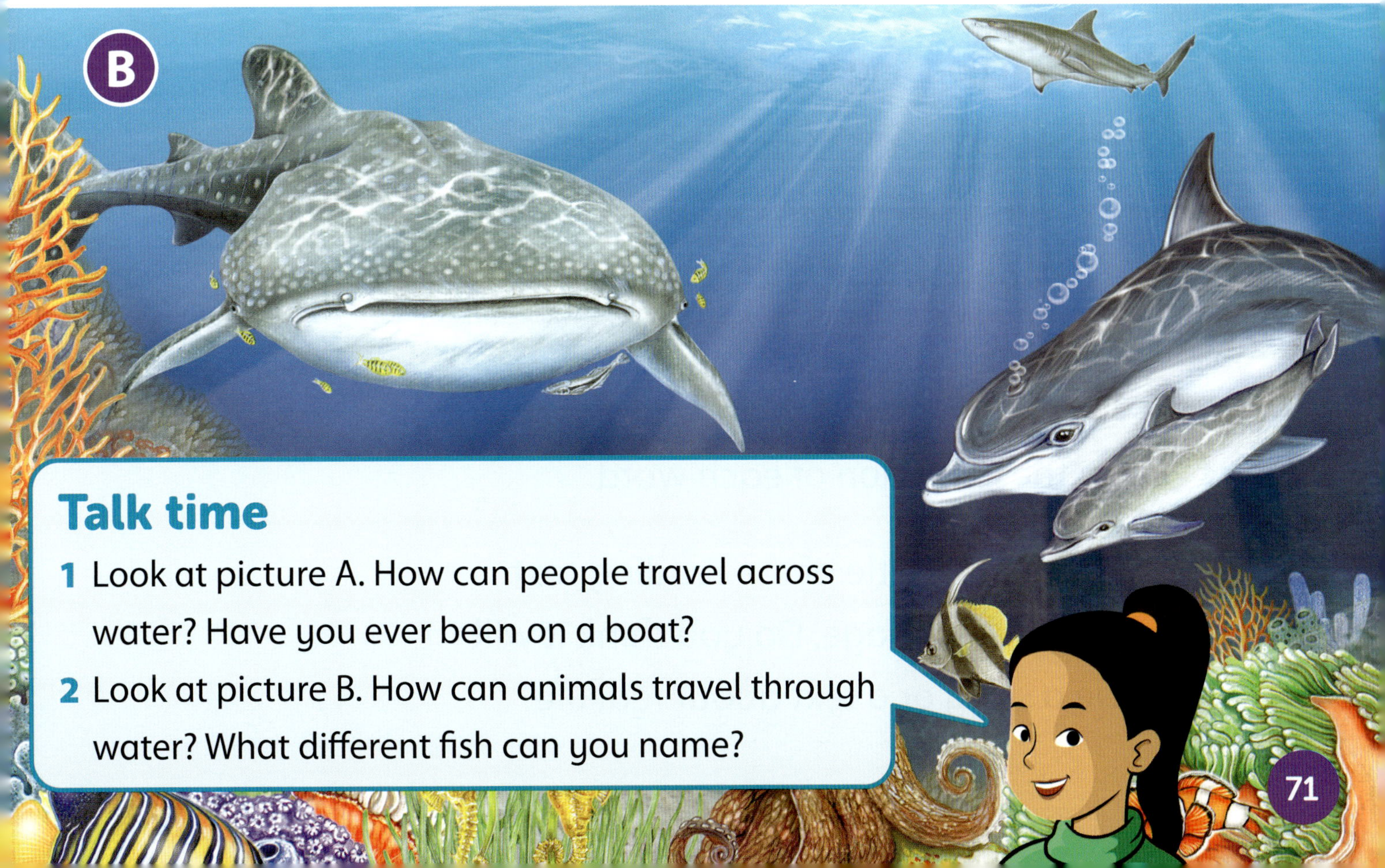

B

Talk time

1 Look at picture A. How can people travel across water? Have you ever been on a boat?

2 Look at picture B. How can animals travel through water? What different fish can you name?

A–Z of the Sea

- Talk about the sea
- Organize words from A–Z
- Use a dictionary

A Words in dictionaries are listed in A–Z order. These pictures are from a book *A–Z of the Sea*. Read each word. Point to the first letter in each word. Write the words in their correct A–Z order.

| shark | whale | fish | coral |

B

1 What can you find in a dictionary? What can you use a dictionary for?

2 Work with a partner to find these words in a dictionary.

fish   fin   gill

3 Copy the definition of each word.

C Look at the title of the reading text on the next page. Do you think it will be a story or a text about real life?

- Read a fact text
- Learn new words
- Use a glossary

Ocean Sharks

What is a shark?

A shark is a fish. Sharks swim in seas all over the world. Some sharks swim in cold seas, some prefer warm seas. Some sharks live close to the **shore**. Some live in deep seas.

Glossary

shore land along the edge of a sea or lake

Parts of a shark

A shark has a tail and fins for swimming. The tail and fins help steer it and stop it from rolling over.

Sharks have a strong sense of smell but cannot see very far.

Gills

Animals need to breathe. We breathe with **lungs**. Sharks breathe with gills.

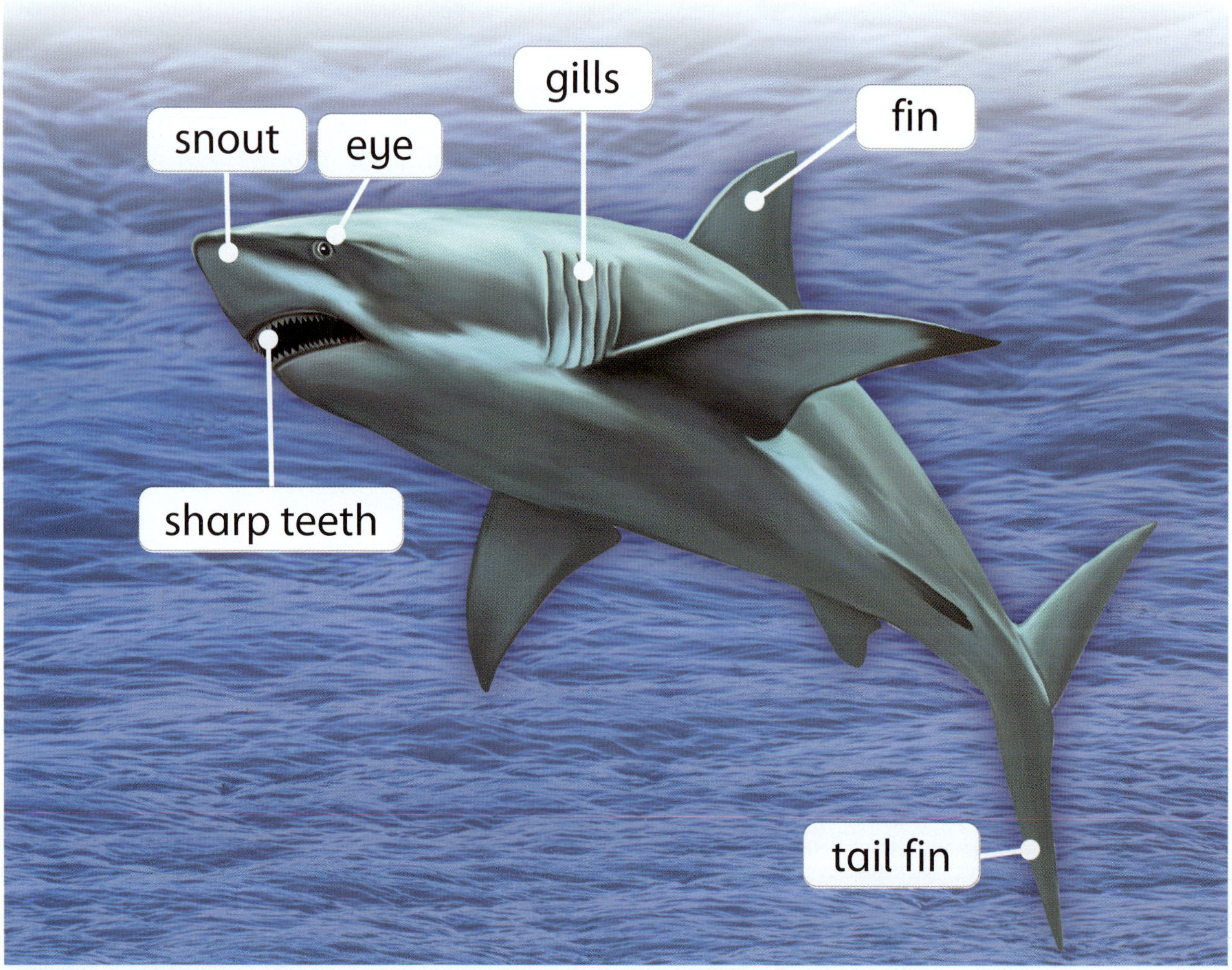

Glossary

lungs parts of the body that help us to breathe

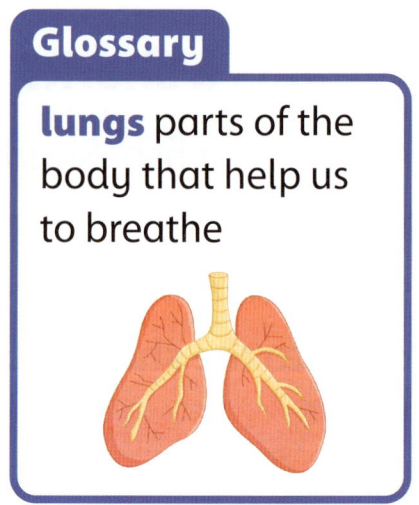

snout

eye

gills

fin

sharp teeth

tail fin

All sorts of sharks

There are many different sorts of sharks. Sharks can be as long as a truck or shorter than an arm. Two of the biggest sharks are the whale shark and the basking shark. The dwarf lantern shark is the smallest. It fits in a person's hand.

dwarf lantern shark

whale shark

basking shark

The whale shark is a gentle giant. Most sharks are very shy of people and will swim away if people go near.

The great white shark is one of the biggest fish in the sea. It **hunts** seals and penguins.

Glossary

hunts chases to kill and eat

Hunting sharks have hundreds of teeth set in rows. They are very sharp and pointed.

- Find information in a text
- Label a picture

A Read and respond

1 What is a shark? Tell a partner.

2 Where do sharks live? Tell a partner.

> **cold oceans**   **warm oceans**
> **both cold and warm oceans**

3 Draw a picture of a shark. Put the labels in the right place on your picture.

eye   teeth   gills   snout

Learning tip
The picture on page 74 will help you.

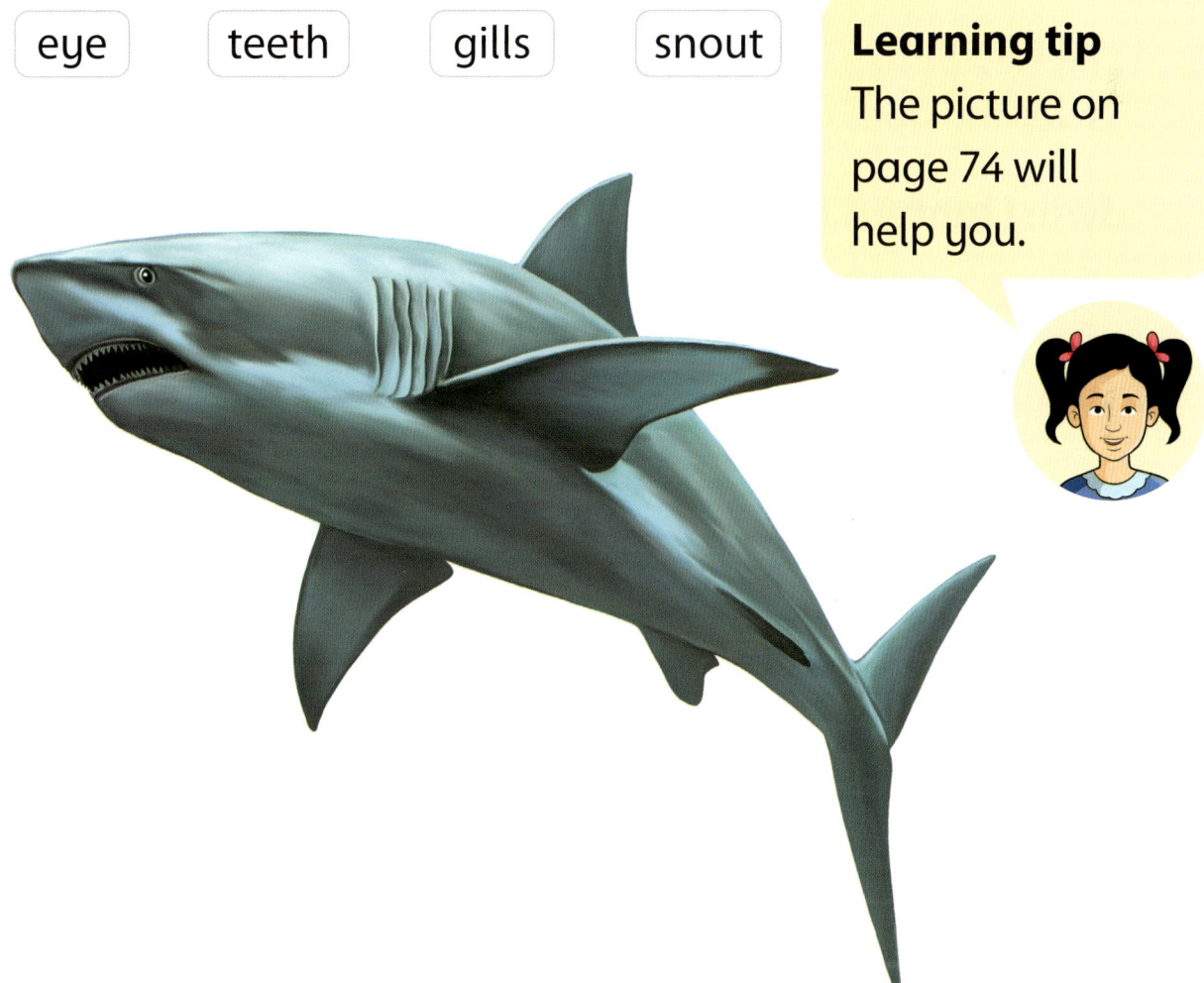

- Talk about sharks
- Write about sharks

B

1 Which of these sentences is true and which is false? Copy the sentences that are true.

Sharks breathe through lungs.

Sharks have a tail fin.

There are only three types of sharks.

Some sharks have hundreds of teeth.

Learning tip
Look at pages 73–76 to help you.

2 Read the names of the sharks and answer the questions with a partner.

**dwarf lantern shark   whale shark
great white shark**

- Which shark eats penguins?
- Which shark is gentle and big?
- Which shark is the smallest?

C What do you think?

1 Which shark would you most like to see? Why? Tell a partner.

2 Write a sentence: **I would like to see a … because … .**

- Find words with **-ing** and **-s**
- Find words with the sound **/sh/**

A

1 Find three words in the text that end with **-ing**. Practise saying them. Write them down.

2 Find three words in the text that end with **-s**. Practise saying them. Write them down.

B

1 Find all the words in the text that have the **/sh/** sound. Practise saying these words.

2 Find these sentences in the text. Copy the sentences and add the missing words.

Two of the _____ sharks are the whale shark and the basking shark.

The dwarf lantern shark is the _____ .

The great white shark is the _____ hunter in the sea.

3 Tell a partner what you notice about the missing words.

Language tip
The sound **/sh/** can be found at the beginning or end of a word, like **sh**ark and ru**sh**.

smallest   biggest

79

• Find verbs in a text

 C

1 Read the words with a partner. Which three words are doing words? Write them down.

> swim   deep   hunt
> breathe   shark

2 Write three more verbs that you know.

3 Use a dictionary to check your spelling.

Language tip
A doing word is called a **verb**.

● **Stretch zone**

1 Write some questions to ask your classmates to see what they remember about sharks and sea travel.

2 Ask at least six people to answer your questions.

- Read a fact text
- Learn new words
- Use a glossary

Sea Transport

There are lots of ways to travel across the sea. Some ways have been used for a long time and some are new.

Paddling

Paddling is the oldest way to cross the water. Thousands of years ago people made boats from big logs or tree trunks. They made paddles to push the boat along.

Kayaks

Nowadays, lots of people paddle small boats called kayaks. Sea kayaks are good for exploring around the coast.

Glossary

canoe long, narrow boat powered by paddles

paddle

canoe

sea kayak

Dragon boats

Dragon boats were first made 2000 years ago in China. They are made from wood. A team of paddlers make dragon boats move fast.

sail

Each boat has a **carved** dragon head at the front.

Glossary

carved cut out of hard material

Ancient Egyptians used boats like this 4500 years ago to sail across the sea.

There is a dragon boat race held at Stanley Beach, Hong Kong. A large crowd of people watch the race each year.

Sailing

Ancient Egyptians and Arabs were the first people to use sails to power their boats and ships.

- Find information in a text
- Talk about a question

A Read and respond

1 Point to the headings in the text. Read them aloud with a partner.

2 Why are headings used in the text? Tell a partner.

B

1 How did people first travel by sea?

> **dragon boat**   **sail boat**
> **paddle boat**

2 When were dragon boats first made? Tell a partner.

> **200 years ago**   **2000 years ago**
> **20 years ago**

Learning tip
200 = two hundred
2000 = two thousand

C What do you think?

Which of these things is the most fun to do in the sea? Share your ideas with a partner.

> **swim**   **kayak**   **paddle**
> **dragon boat**   **sail**

?

How can we help to look after the sea?

- Label a picture
- Find and spell words with **-ing**

A Write the correct labels for this picture.

kayak   paddle   kayaker

1

2

3

B

1 One word in each sentence needs an **-ing** ending. Write the words with the **-ing** ending.

Paddle is the oldest way to cross the water.

Sea kayaks are good for explore around the coast.

2 Talk with a partner. What did you have to take off to add the **-ing** ending?

Language tip
If a verb ends in **-e**, you have to take off the **-e** to add **-ing**.

Part 1

1 Copy the sentence about sharks. Choose two words to fill the gaps.

Sharks are found in _____ seas and in _____ seas.

> **cold   swim   shore   gills**
> **warm   teeth**

2 Write two more sentences about sharks. Try to use some of the words in the box above.

3 Write two sentences about boats. Try to use some of the words in the box below.

> **pull   float   coast   push   sails**

Part 2

1 Draw and label a picture of a dragon boat. Use the words in the box to help you.

> **dragon head   paddle**
> **wood**

Puff!

One puff, two puffs, three puffs, four
Five puffs, six puffs –
You can't see me any more!

Liz Miles

Talk time

1 Do you have a favourite animal? Is it real, or imaginary?
2 Why is this your favourite animal?

- Read a poem
- Talk about a poem
- Find information in a poem
- Find words that rhyme

A Read and respond

1 What hides the dragon? Tell a partner.

one puff   six puffs   four puffs

2 Which words rhyme in the poem? Point to the rhyming words and say them with a partner.

B Which words from the list have the same sound? Tell a partner.

two   see   more   four   you   me

C What do you think?

1 Where do the puffs come from?
- the wind
- the dragon's breath
- a fire

2 Learn the poem and say it aloud with a partner.

Language tip
In a poem, the **rhyming words** are at the end of a line.

Learning tip
Read the words aloud to hear which sound the same.

- Read a poem
- Learn new words
- Use a glossary

Late One Night in Kalamazoo

Late one night in Kalamazoo,
the baboons had a barbeque,
the **kudus** flew a green balloon,
the poodles **yodelled** to the moon.

A monkey strummed a blue guitar;
a donkey caught a falling star,
a camel danced with a kangaroo,
late one night in Kalamazoo.

Jack Prelutsky

Glossary

kudu a large, white-striped antelope or deer with long horns

yodelled sang in an up-and-down voice

- Find information in a poem
- Talk about verbs

A Read and respond

1 What colour was the balloon in the poem?

2 Draw the balloon, then colour it in.

3 Can you find another colour in the poem? Tell a partner.

B What did each animal do in the poem? Tell a partner.

camel   **monkey**

poodles   **baboons**

> **yodelled   danced   had a barbeque
> strummed a guitar**

C

1 What is the name for a doing word?

2 Look at the words for what each animal did.

3 Write down the verbs.

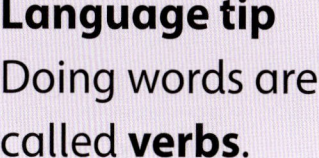
Language tip
Doing words are called **verbs**.

89

● Find words with the sound **/oo/**

A

1 Which four animals in the poem have an **/oo/** sound? Write them down.

> **baboon   kangaroo   camel
> kudu   donkey   poodle**

Language tip
In the word **kudu** the letter **u** makes an **/oo/** sound.

2 Which other words in the poem have **/oo/** sounds? Practise saying them with a partner.

B Find five words from the poem in the wordsearch.

> **balloon   kangaroo   poodle
> moon   baboon**

b	a	l	l	o	o	n	r
a	p	o	o	d	l	e	t
b	g	m	d	l	e	b	f
n	t	o	l	t	e	a	d
m	o	o	f	r	c	b	g
k	a	n	g	a	r	o	o
s	v	a	m	a	h	o	l
t	b	n	r	s	f	n	k

- Read a poem
- Learn new words
- Use a glossary

A Hatchling's Song

I'm almost **hatched**!
I'm almost hatched!
I'm small, I'm wet,
I'm not out yet.
I'm almost hatched!

I'm pecking hard,
I'm pecking hard.
I'm tired, I'm weak,
It hurts my beak.
I'm pecking hard.

Glossary

hatchling a baby bird that has just come out of the egg

hatched newly born out of an egg

My head's outside,
My head's outside.
The moon is bright –
The world's so white!
My head's outside.

I'm really hatched,
I'm really hatched.
At last I'm free.
Hey, Dad, it's me!
I'm really hatched.

Judy Sierra

- Find information in a poem
- Talk about a poem

A Read and respond

1 Who is speaking in the poem?

2 Tell a partner how you know.

> **Dad   Mum   a hatchling**

Learning tip
Think about who **I** is in the poem.

B Write the sentences in the order they happen in the poem.

The hatchling's head is out.

The hatchling pecks hard.

The hatchling is free.

The hatchling hurts its beak.

C What do you think?

1 How do you think the hatchling feels at the end of the poem? Talk with a partner.

> **cross and tired   upset
> happy and tired**

2 Why do you think the hatchling feels this way? Tell a partner.

● Find words with **-ed** and **-ing**

A Find a word in the poem with an **-ed** ending and one with an **-ing** ending. Write them down.

B Write the words again without the **-ing** and **-ed** endings.

Language tip
Taking the **-ed** from **cracked** makes **crack**.

Stretch zone

1 Look around you. Imagine you are like the baby penguin, seeing the world for the first time.

2 What would look exciting? What would look beautiful? What would look strange? Talk to a partner.

3 Write some words to describe what you see.

Tiny Diny

Dear, oh dear,
oh, what shall I do?
There's a tiny little dinosaur
in my shoe.

Her teeth are sharp
and her head's like a rock
When I put my foot in,
she chewed my sock.

- Learn new words
- Use a glossary
- Talk about a poem

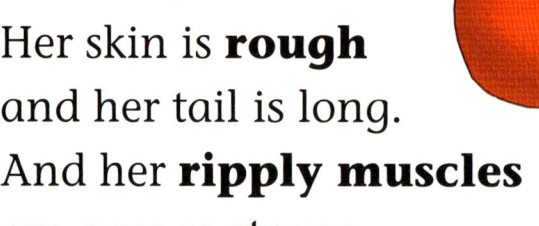

Her skin is **rough**
and her tail is long.
And her **ripply muscles**
are ever so strong.

And I want to go out,
but what can I do
with a tiny little dinosaur
in my shoe?

Tony Mitton

Talk time

1 How would you feel if you found a tiny dinosaur in your shoe?

2 What would you do?

Glossary

rough having an uneven surface

ripply rising and falling

muscles fleshy parts of the body that help an animal move

- Use describing words
- Find words with **sh**
- Talk about a question

 A **Read and respond**

Why does the poet call the tiny dinosaur **Diny**? Tell a partner.

B

1   Read and copy the nouns.

muscles   **skin**

teeth   **tail**

2   Write a word to describe each noun next to it.

sharp   ripply   long   rough

Language tip
Words that describe things are called **adjectives**.

C   Find words in the poem that begin with **sh**. Write the words.

?

Why is it important for parents to care for their babies? What sort of things do your parents teach you?

- Copy a poem
- Write rhyming words

Copy the rhyming poem below. Use the words in the box to complete the poem. Then read it aloud to a partner.

goes	tough	shoe	toes

Never fear
Here's what to do
If a tiny diny
Jumps in your … .

Do not cry
If its skin is rough
Do not scream
If it's big and … .

Pull off its socks
And tickle its …
Quick as a flash
Away it … !

Stretch zone

1 Draw pictures to tell a story about a child who finds a baby dinosaur.
2 Tell the story to a partner. How does the child feel? What is the dinosaur like? What do they do together?

7 Stories about our world

Talk time

1 Do you ever go out at night?

2 How is night-time different from the daytime? What can you see? What can you hear?

- Read a story
- Talk about night-time
- Learn new words
- Use a glossary

The Lost Stars

Hannah Cumming

The world is a bright, busy place, full of noise.

The lights are always on. People are always talking and moving.

They switch things on and they watch things and they do things, night and day.

They are so busy, that often they forget to stop and look up.

But I don't see anything!

Exactly!

Every night, the stars come out and go to work in the sky. They are beautiful to see, and **proud** to shine in the sky every night.

Glossary

proud pleased with something

fed up cross, annoyed or miserable

smog dirty air made of smoke and fog

break a short rest

But they are getting **fed up**. The light and the **smog** stop people from seeing the stars.

The stars have had enough. They are taking a **break**.

In the meantime, the world is getting busier.

More and more lights go on …

… louder and louder …

… brighter and brighter …

… until …

… suddenly …

The power runs out. Everyone is in the dark!

Glossary

remember to think of something and not forget it

A Read and respond

1 What do the people forget to do? Write it down.

> **They forget to turn on the lights.**
> **They forget to stop and look up.**
> **They forget to talk.**

2 On page 102, why can't the people see anything in the sky? Tell a partner.

B

1 Why has the power run out? Tell a partner.

2 How do the people feel? How do the stars feel? Tell a partner.

> **annoyed   fed up   tired   confused**

C What do you think?

Tell a partner what you think will happen next in the story.

- Read a story
- Learn new words
- Use a glossary

A few remember the light of the stars.
They set off to track them down.
They search everywhere.

Sometimes, they think they have found the stars.

But it's not really them.

Finally, far away, they come across a beach. Could it be?

They have found the lost stars! They **beg** them to come back, but the stars are not sure.

Glossary

beg to ask someone very strongly to do something

Come back!

We'll be good.

Please!

Finally, the stars agree, but only if people promise not to forget them again.

The stars had missed the night sky, and all of the people, too.

Everyone made sure that they would never forget to look up at night again!

- Talk about feelings
- Find information in a story

A Read and respond

1 Why do the stars feel fed up? Tell a partner.

2 Why do the people set off to track down the stars? Tell a partner.

B Write down the two sentences that are true.

The light and smog were beautiful.

People could not see the stars.

The stars made the power go off.

The world got louder and brighter.

Learning tip
Read the story that starts on page 100 to help you.

109

● Describe the night sky

C What do you think?

1 At the end of the story, the stars light the night. What would you do in the starlight? Tell a partner.

2 What do you think the star is thinking in this picture? Write a sentence to show what the star is thinking.

3 Can you see the stars at night where you live? Draw a picture to show what you can see at night.

- Use capital letters and full stops
- Find compound words
- Use long vowel sounds

A Copy these sentences. Change the letters that should be capital letters and add the full stop.

> **i don't see anything!**

> **they could give us light**

B

1 Find three words in the story that are made up of two words. Write them down.

2 Draw a line in each word to show the two words within it. For example: **every/where**.

C Copy these sentences. Write **ea**, **ee**, **y**, **igh** or **oo** to finish the words.

We can't s＿＿ them!

Ever＿＿ night, the stars come out.

They came across a b＿＿ch.

The stars had missed the n＿＿＿t

sky, and all the people, t＿＿.

Language tip
Compound words are made by joining two words together:
star + light = starlight
every + where = everywhere

111

Part 1

Look at the pictures and read the sentences.
Write the sentences in the order they happen
in the story. Look back at the story to help you.

The people set off to track down the stars.

The power runs out!

The stars come out and go to work.

The people will never forget to look up at night again.

The stars take a break.

The people find the stars!

- Retell a story
- Talk about a question

Part 2

Use the pictures and sentences in Part 1 to retell the story to a partner.

Listen to a partner retell the story to you.

?

1 **Do you think it is important to look at the stars? Why? Why not?**
2 **What other things in nature do you look at?**

Stretch zone

1 What would happen if something in nature suddenly disappeared, like the sun or the rain, or trees?
2 Draw pictures to show what might happen.

8 About my life

Talk time

1 Which places do you like visiting?
2 Do you like going on holiday?
3 Tell a partner about your best holiday ever.

A Have you ever moved house? What do you think it might be like to move house? Tell a partner about it.

- Talk about your experiences
- Listen to others
- Talk about things that are important to you

B

1 Imagine you moved house and could only take three things with you. Tell a partner what you would take.

2 Say why these things are most important to you.

3 Draw a picture of each thing and write the word.

- Read a recount text
- Learn new words
- Use a glossary

My First Year in Vietnam was Weird

D'Arcy Hipgrave (aged 7)

from *Slurping Soup and Other Confusions:*
www.slurpingsoup.com

When I left **Melbourne** in Australia to live in **Hanoi** in Vietnam it was really **weird**.

I missed the traffic lights in Melbourne. There were no traffic lights in Hanoi, so mad motorbikes were everywhere, even on the footpaths!

Glossary

Melbourne big city in Australia
Hanoi capital city of Vietnam
weird strange

Traffic in Hanoi

Another thing I missed was playing **footy**.

I felt shy at school. I didn't like the first year.

In the second year I went to a French school. But learning to speak French was hard, so I wanted to go back to the English school. I think I was a bit mixed up.

Glossary

footy a short word for football

Learning tip
A **recount text** is a text someone writes about something that they did.

Me on a trip to Sapa in northern Vietnam

Me in noisy Hanoi!

Later on that year, I met Jono, another **Aussie**.

My French got better, and then I felt very happy.

Now I can speak French and some **Vietnamese**. I love Vietnamese food. I have friends from Vietnam and many other countries. Vietnam is my home and it is not at all weird.

Vietnamese *pho* soup

Glossary

Aussie a person from Australia

Vietnamese from Vietnam, or the language people speak in Vietnam

• Find information in a text

A Read and respond

1 Where did D'Arcy move from?

> **Melbourne   Hanoi   London**

2 Where did he move to? Tell a partner.

3 What two things does D'Arcy say he missed? Tell a partner.

> **traffic   footpaths   traffic lights**
> **football   motorbikes**

4 What do people like to drive in Vietnam?

Language tip
We use **capital letters** for the names of cities, countries and languages.

- **Talk to a partner about your country and other countries**

B

1 How did D'Arcy feel when he first moved house?

> **shy   confident   confused
> weird   happy**

2 What made D'Arcy feel happy again? Name two things.

C What do you think?

1 Would you like to live in another country? Where would you choose?

2 What would be good about life there?

3 What would you miss about home? Tell a partner.

A Copy the sentence below. Add capital letters and a full stop where they are needed.

learning to speak french was hard, so i wanted to go back to the english school

B

1 Read these sentences aloud with a partner.

I can speak French. I can speak a bit of Vietnamese.

2 Where could you put **and**?

3 Copy the sentences. Add **and** in the right place.

C

1 Find three compound words in the text. Copy them down.

2 Draw a line through each word to show the two words within it. Example: **rain/bow**.

- Use capital letters and full stops
- Join sentences with **and**
- Find compound words

Learning tip Compound words are made by joining two words together. Example: football

?

Moving house is a challenging experience. What have you done that is challenging or made you feel nervous? What did you do to feel better?

- Read about someone's life
- Read new words
- Use a glossary

Alex Brychta – a Biography

Introduction

Alex Brychta draws and paints pictures for stories. The stories are about three children, called Biff, Chip and Kipper. Lots of children read the stories and love Alex's **illustrations**.

Alex has drawn Biff, Chip and Kipper thousands of times!

Glossary

biography story of a person's life
illustrations pictures in a book

Alex in his art studio

Learning tip
Captions
give more information about pictures.

Biff (girl) has a twin brother called Chip. Kipper is their younger brother. They have a dog called Floppy.

Alex's childhood

Alex was born in the city of Prague – the capital of the Czech Republic.

Alex's parents were artists, so Alex did lots of drawing as a little boy. When he was older he drew cartoons.

Learning tip
Non-fiction texts use **headings** to organize information.

Three-year-old Alex

Alex was ten years old when he did this cartoon.

● Find information in a text

A Read and respond

1 What is Alex's job? Write it down.

> **author   doctor   illustrator**

2 How many times has Alex drawn Floppy?

> **300   30 000   1 000 000+**

B

1 Where was Alex born? Write it down.

2 What did his parents do for a job? Write it down.

C What do you think?

1 Do you think Alex enjoys his job? Tell a partner.

2 Have you read any books about Biff, Chip, Kipper and Floppy the dog?

Learning tip
Look at page 123 to find out about Alex's parents.

- Read about someone's life

A new country

In 1968, Alex's mum and dad told Alex and his sister that they must leave their country.

One night, the family packed their bags and set off in the car. After a long **journey**, the family got to England to start a new life. Alex was twelve years old.

Glossary

journey going from one place to another

The family escaped from their country.

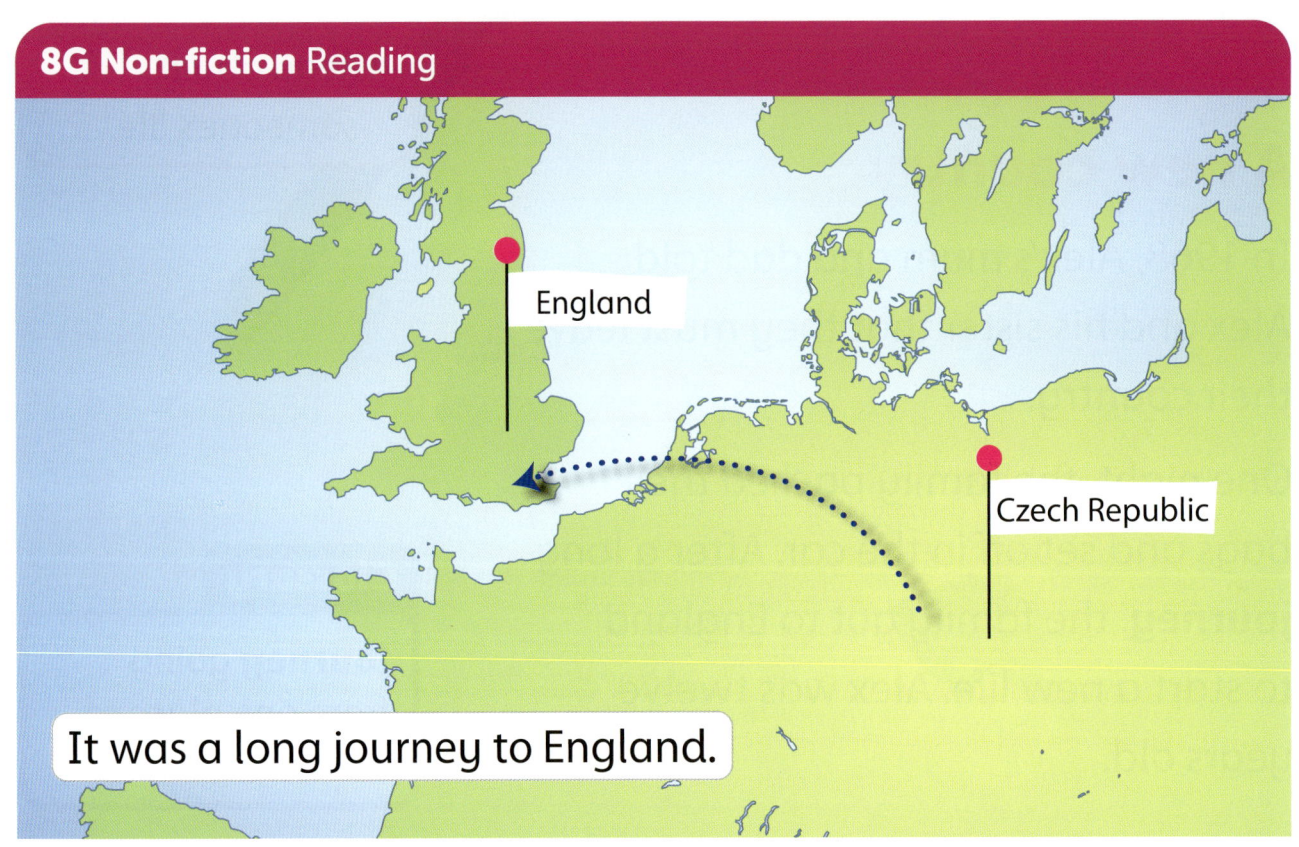

England

Czech Republic

It was a long journey to England.

In England

At first, Alex could not understand English. He drew lots of pictures at school and did not listen to the teachers. A teacher told him off. But the teacher looked at his drawings. He said, "Alex, these are very good and look like book illustrations."

Biff, Chip and Kipper

In 1984, Alex illustrated the first story about Biff, Chip and Kipper.

Alex with his sister, mum and dad in England

● Find information in a text

 Read and respond

Write down the sentences which are true.

The family left home in the daytime.

Alex's teacher did not like his drawings.

Alex could not understand English.

B

1 How old was Alex when he moved to England? Write it down.
2 Who did Alex move to England with? Write it down.

Learning tip
Read page 125 to find the answer.

C **What do you think?**

What two experiences do Alex and D'Arcy share? Tell a partner.

- Spell words with **-s**, **-ing** and **-ed**
- Use capital letters and full stops
- Make opposites with **un-**

A Write the sentence below. Add the missing **-s**, **-ing** and **-ed** endings to the words with gaps.

Alex has illustrate _____ lot _____ of children's read _____ books.

B

1 Rewrite the sentence. Add three capital letters and a full stop.

at first, alex could not understand english

2 Now write a sentence of your own about Alex. Use at least one capital letter and a full stop.

C Choose the right word to complete the sentences.

At first, D'Arcy felt ... (happy/unhappy)

When he made friends he felt ... (happy/unhappy)

Alex was very ... at drawing (confident/unconfident)

Language tip
If a word already ends in **-e**, you only need to add **-d** not **-ed**.

Language tip
We can make some words mean the opposite by adding **un-**.
happy 😊
unhappy 🙁

- Write about a difficult time
- Write a short story

Part 1

1 Tell a partner about something you found difficult. Perhaps it was trying a new food, meeting someone new, going on stage or going to the dentist.

2 Now write some sentences about the event. Use the sentence starters to help you.

It was difficult for me when …

I found … difficult because …

3 Write a sentence about what you did to overcome the difficulty.

Part 2

1 Write a short story about a person or an animal who moves house.

2 Share your writing with a partner.

3 Say what you like about your partner's writing and how to make it even better.

Stretch zone

1 What do you know about your parent or carer's life? Tell a partner.

2 Write three sentences about your mother, father, carer or grandparent, and their life.

3 Use 'and' to join ideas in one sentence.

4 Share your writing with a partner. Check their work.

Off We Go to Mexico!

Laurie Krebs

Off we go, off we go, off we go to Mexico!

We swim in turquoise water and build castles on the beach.
We climb up rocks or watch from **docks**,
To see the grey whales **breach**.

We hop aboard the **canyon** train. Across the bridge we go.
Up mountains steep, through tunnels deep,
We dare not look below.

Glossary

docks part of a harbour where ships are loaded or unloaded

breach to leap from the water

canyon deep valley which may have a river running through it

- Read a poem
- Use a glossary
- Talk about travelling

We hurry to a festival held in the village
square. There's food to eat and friends
  to meet
And laughter everywhere.

We climb amazing pyramids from
  ancient Mexico
And wonder how they're standing now
When built so long ago.

Talk time

1 If you could go anywhere you wished,
where would you go?

2 Who would you go with?

3 What would you do there?

131

We **trek** to native villages, for this is market day.
Their rich supply of things to buy
Creates a bright display.

Glossary

trek to take a long walk

Find information in a poem
Choose adjectives

A Read and respond

1 Which country are the family visiting?
Write it down.

2 What do they climb up rocks to see?
Write it down.

**the beach   the docks   whales
the market**

B What do the family do at the festival?
Tell a partner.

C What do you think?

The writer describes the market as 'bright'.
Choose two other words to describe
the market.

**quiet   dull   busy   exciting
colourful   empty   fun**

Language tip
Words used to describe things are called **adjectives**.

We circle round the plaza and we hear the stamping feet.
As dancers **twirl**, their costumes swirl
To the guitarists' beat.

We **hike** up to the winter home of the monarch butterflies.
When sunshine brings a burst of wings,
Their glitter fills the skies.

Glossary

twirl to spin around
hike to go for a long walk in the countryside

134

We wander through the capital, where there's so much to see:

The park, the zoo, museums too,
And **Aztec** history.

Glossary

Aztec to do with ancient Mexico

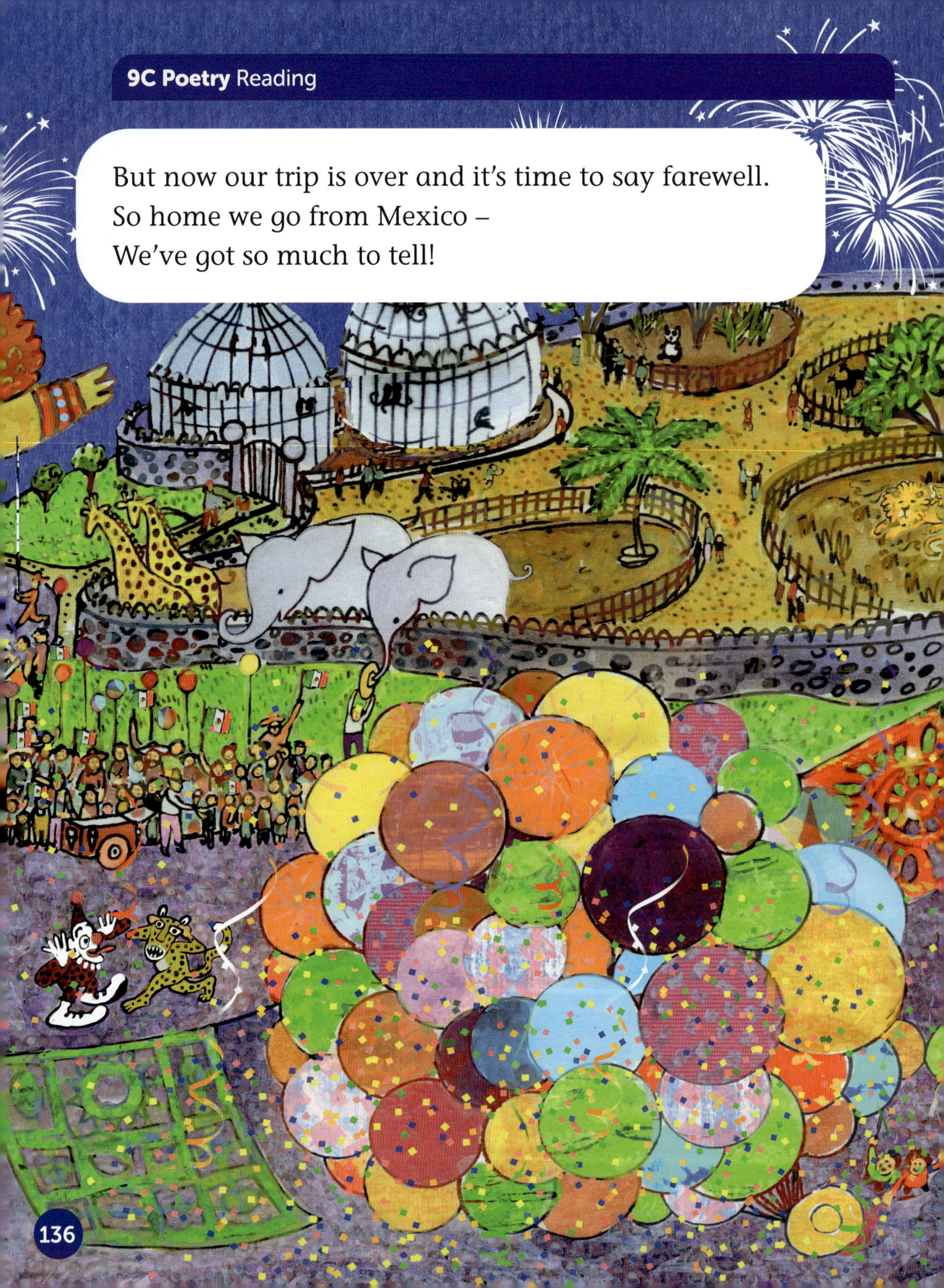

But now our trip is over and it's time to say farewell.
So home we go from Mexico –
We've got so much to tell!

● Find information in a poem

A Read and respond

1 What two things do the family hear at the plaza? Write them down.

> **butterflies dancers museums
> guitarists**

2 Read the sentences below. Write them in the order they happen in the poem.

We see butterflies.

Home we go from Mexico.

Off we go to Mexico!

We climb amazing pyramids.

3 What makes the butterflies want to fly? Tell a partner.

- Talk about a poem

B

1 How many different places in Mexico did the family visit?

2 Write down each place you can remember.

3 Look at a partner's list to check if you have forgotten any places.

Learning tip
A section of a poem is called a **verse** or a **stanza**.

C What do you think?

Read the verse from the poem that you like best to a partner. Explain why you like it.

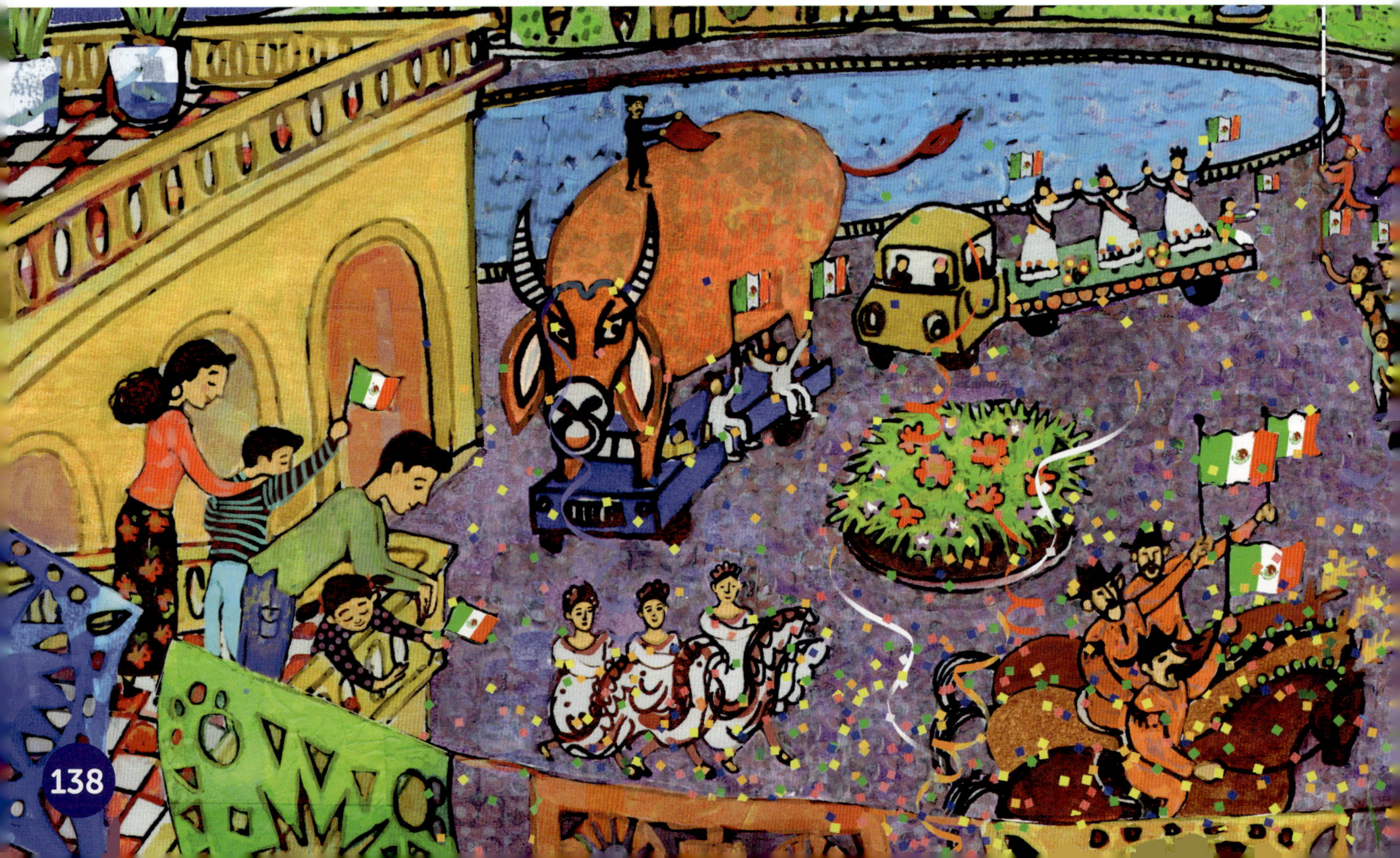

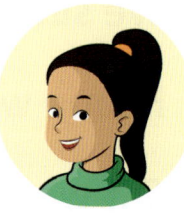

● Find rhyming
 words
● Use verbs

A With a partner, find a rhyming word from the poem for each of the words below.

> beach   steep   eat   twirl
> feet   day   zoo

Language tip
Words that **rhyme** sound the same, like **fun** and **run**.

B

1 Copy the words below. Add in the first letter of each word to show some of the things the family did on holiday.

> _limb _wim _rek _ike _ander

2 Choose two of the verbs above. Use them to write two sentences about what the family did in Mexico.

139

Part 1

Look at these pictures of things to do on holiday.

1 What are the people doing in each picture? Talk about it with a partner.

2 Choose three of these activities that you would like to put in a poem.

Part 2

1 Think about your best holiday ever or somewhere you would like to go. Talk with a partner about it.

2 Write some words to describe your holiday. Use some of the words from the poem to help you.
Can you think of any rhyming words to use in your poem?

3 Write a short poem about your perfect holiday.

Stretch zone

Read your poem aloud to a partner and talk about it. Tell a partner:

- two things you like about their poem
- one way they could make it even better.

- Use rhyming words
- Write a short poem
- Talk about a question

Language tip
Here are some more **rhyming** words to help you:
sun fun see me tree free sea walk talk play day say may

?

Is it important to visit new places?
Can you think of a memory you have of going somewhere new?

Read this non-fiction text about how spacecraft use electricity, before reading the story, *Glimmer* on p144.

Energy in Space

Spacecraft need electricity, so that their lights and computers will work. But how do they get it? They use solar panels. When sunlight hits the **solar panels**, the solar panels make electricity. This electricity is stored in batteries.

> **Glossary**
>
> **solar panels** panels that get energy from the sun

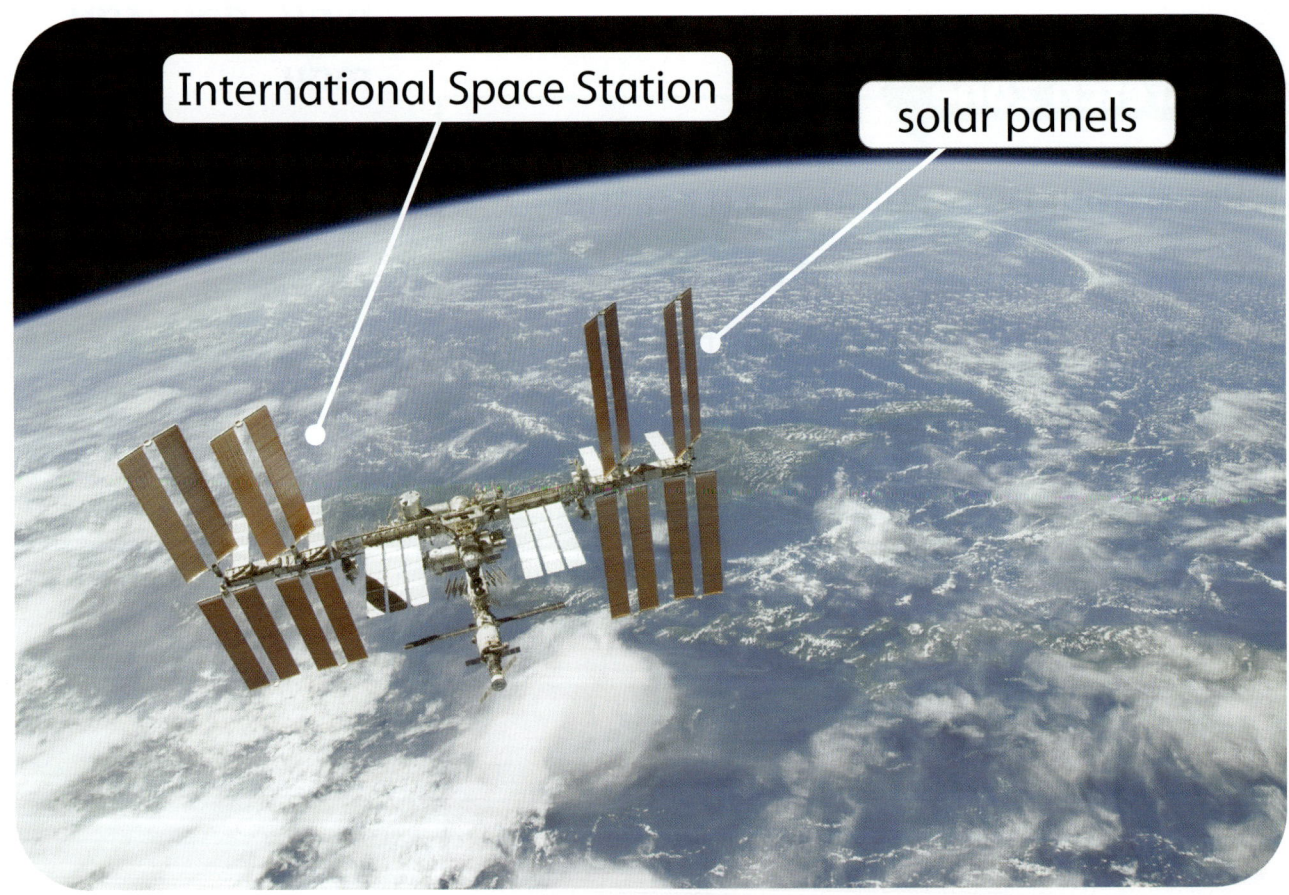

International Space Station

solar panels

If the solar panels stopped working, the batteries would give the spacecraft electricity for a while. But the lights might go dim. This would help save energy for more important things – like making sure there is air for the astronauts to breathe.

Glimmer

Written by Becca Heddle

Illustrated by Joe Todd-Stanton

I was on a long space trip with my family. One day, we suddenly saw a trader ship. Trader ships are a bit like shops in space.

My big brother, Jax, **groaned**. "Do we have to go shopping?"

But my little brother, Tad, was excited.

Glossary

groaned made a low sound to show disappointment

Talk time

1 Where were the family?
2 Why did Jax groan?
3 What are trader ships?

145

Mum and Dad spent ages deciding what to buy.

When they were finally paying, one of the traders gave me a bag.

"You look bored," he said. "This will brighten things up." He smiled.

As we zoomed away from the trader ship, something banged into our solar panels. All the lights went **dim**, to save power.

Glossary

dim not very bright

"Let's get our spacesuits on," Mum said to Dad.
"We need to fix those panels."

Jax walked off, but Tad stayed with me. He doesn't like the dark.

To take Tad's mind off his **fears**, I felt inside the trader's bag. I found a little ball. It squeaked, **sprang** out of my hand and rolled away!

Glossary

fears feeling that something bad is going to happen
sprang jumped up

Tad jumped. "What was that?" he said.

"I think that ball is alive," I said. "Help me find it before Mum and Dad come back."

We started looking all over the dimly lit ship.

Tad found the ball. He's got very **sharp eyes**. It was definitely alive!

Glossary

sharp eyes eyes which see things easily

Talk time

1 How does Tad feel about being in the dark?

2 What do you think the ball is?

3 Do you think the ball is really alive?

The ball creature was hiding behind a seat. When we came near, it **shrank** away from us.

Glossary

shrank got smaller

"It's scared," said Tad. "Can you help it?"

I sat near the creature and held out my hand.

The ball slowly rolled closer until it was touching my hand. And it started to **glow**!

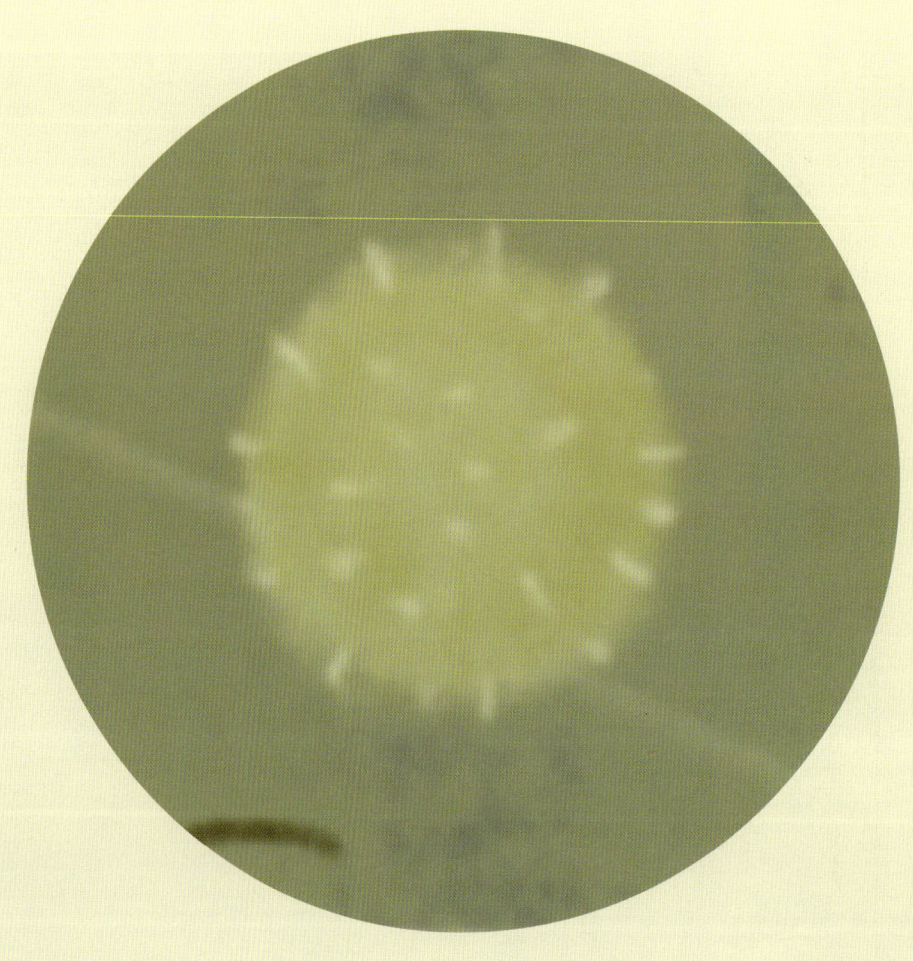

Glossary

glow shine with a warm light

I gently picked up the creature and stroked it. It glowed brighter – and got bigger.

Jax finally noticed us. "Wow – you've got a glimmer!" he said. "It must like you. Glimmers only glow when they're happy."

Mum and Dad came in.

"Sorry, guys," sighed Mum. "We'll be stuck with dim lights until we can get the solar panels mended properly."

Talk time

1 How do you think the children feel about being in the dark?

2 Is it good that the children have a glimmer? Why?

"Mum, I think our new pet can help!" I said.

The glimmer glowed and glowed – and Mum brightened up at once.

My story review

- Write a story review
- Talk about a question

Complete this sentence about *Glimmer*.

The part of the story I liked best was … .

Would you tell your friends to read this story? Why? Why not?

Draw your favourite part of the story.

?

In the story, Tad was afraid of the dark. Are you afraid of anything?

Language tip
A **review** is when you say whether you like something or not, and what you like about it. We write it in the past tense: **I liked … it was …**